Discovery House Publishers

Books, music, and videos that feed the soul with the Word of God

Box 3566 Grand Rapids, MI 49501

A CONSPICUOUS LOVE

The Enduring Story of
Ruth, Romance & Redemption

Steve Zeisler

A Conspicuous Love
© 1999 by Steve Zeisler. All rights reserved.

Discovery House is affiliated with RBC Ministries, Grand
Rapids, Michigan, 49512.

Discovery House books are distributed to the trade exclusively
by Barbour Publishing, Inc., Uhrichsville, Ohio 44683.

Unless otherwise indicated, Scripture is taken from the HOLY BIBLE:
NEW INTERNATIONAL VERSION. © 1973, 1978, 1984 by the
International Bible Society. Used by permission of Zondervan Bible
Publishers.

Library of Congress Cataloging-in-Publication Data

Zeisler, Steve, 1949–
    A conspicuous love : the enduring story of Ruth, romance &
redemption / Steve Zeisler.
        p.   cm.
    ISBN 1-57293-040-3
    1. Bible. O.T. Ruth—Commentaries. I. Title.
BS1315.3.Z45   1998
222'.3507—dc21   98-43634
                                                        CIP

Printed in the United States of America

99 01 03 02 00
CHG
1 3 5 7 9 8 6 4 2

CONTENTS

CHAPTER 1

AN OLD STORY
OF NEW TRUTHS

Overview of the book of Ruth

Personally, I have no interest in romance novels. You know the kind I mean: The cover depicts a woman with a dreamy expression and half-closed eyes, in a clinch with a fellow with a strong chin, shoulder-length hair, torn shirt, and the rippling biceps of a construction worker. The blurb under the title reads, "When she was in his arms, nothing mattered—not even his terrible secret!" (If that is *your* kind of book, no offense intended.)

The book of Ruth *is* a romance story—but it is hardly a Harlequin or Silhouette romance novel. The beauty and value of this romance story is that it is *not* just a story for the romance devotee. It is a story that is as powerful and compelling for men as for women. It addresses issues of character, faith, friendship, and relationships in a way that appeals equally to both genders. It speaks to our time as powerfully as it spoke to the era in which it was written.

Yes, it has all the drama and fairy-tale beauty of a well-crafted novel—but this story has the added advantage of being *true*. It is true in the sense that it actually happened during a very real time in human history. It is true in the sense that it contains living, relevant truth that you and I can apply to our lives in the here and now. And it is true in the sense that it embodies rich, eternal truth about the nature of God's relationship with us and the entire human race.

As you begin your study of the story of Ruth, I urge you to read the book through at least once—or better yet, several times in several versions. It's a short book and it lends itself to reading and re-reading, for there are many layers of meaning to explore. As you read, use your imagination. Put yourself in the place of Ruth, Naomi, and Boaz. Imagine the setting. Breathe in the fragrances and touch the textures of a time and place that is so different from our own—yet surprisingly very similar and familiar.

Although the story of Ruth is some three thousand years old, it is a contemporary story, with people you can relate to and identify with to a much greater degree than most of the people you see on your TV set every night. The tensions between the various characters in this story are exactly the same as we experience in relationships today. The people in this story may not be able to fly from coast to coast in five hours, nor can they "surf" the Internet, but those are purely surface differences. Beneath it all, they are people with dreams of home, family, and security, people who fall in love, people who worry about finances and the future, people who sometimes have trouble getting along with each other or trouble communicating with each other. Deep down, human beings haven't really changed in three thousand years— which is why the Bible remains such a relevant book today. The essential truths of the Bible apply in all times and all cultures, including our own.

Today, you can go into any bookstore and find dozens of books filled with advice on romance, relationships, and sexuality—most of it *bad* advice. But in this three thousand year old book, you can find the *best* advice—God's advice—for building a romantic relationship that will last a lifetime. A story that can remain relevant, practical, and full of insight after so many years is worth reading, re-reading, and studying.

You may notice, as you journey through this study in the book of Ruth, that I have not structured this book in the usual Bible commentary style. That is, I don't break the book of Ruth down into chunks of verses and comment on them section by section. That's because the book of Ruth has several layers of meaning, and I want us to explore this book layer by layer. For example, I take three chapters just to examine Ruth chapter 2, because in order to appreciate the various layers of meaning in chapter 2, we have to look at it from three different angles. The book of Ruth is fascinating to explore from any number of angles—as a dramatic and tender love story, rich in emotion and entertainment value; as a parable about the way God works in human lives and human hearts, rich in meaning for our own lives today; and as a foreshadowing of the redemptive work of Jesus Christ, rich in spiritual value for our eternal life with Him.

The book of Ruth has always been regarded as a great work of literature, even by skeptics who don't think the Bible is divinely inspired. It begins with famine and death, and it ends with harvest and birth. So it is a story of redemption and transformation—and therein lies the relevance of this story to your life and mine, even if we are not looking for advice on romance, courtship, and marriage. We all need to experience redemption and God's transforming love—and this book points the way. Embedded in the story of Ruth is a beautiful image of the Redeemer who has been sent to us by a loving God.

The healing power of a good story

Have you ever wondered why God tells so many stories, like the story of Ruth, in His Word? There are certainly many reasons. Stories get our attention (we all love a good story!). Stories instruct (the moral of a good story can stay in our memory for a lifetime). Stories illustrate and bring to life important spiritual principles (which is why most of Jesus' teaching was actually in the form of stories rather than didactic lessons).

But I believe the stories of the Bible serve yet another crucial function in our spiritual journey: Stories bring healing. You may be feeling spiritually sluggish or listless right now. You may even be feeling spiritually nauseous or sin-sick. If so, then the book of Ruth can act as a powerful spiritual medicine in your life right now.

As you know, a physical illness tends to dull your appetite for health. When you're socked in with the flu, the easiest thing to do is pull the covers over your head, draw the curtains, and isolate yourself in a darkened room. Feeling sick makes you avoid the sunlight, fresh air, nourishment, and liquids that actually encourage health to return sooner. The congestion that comes with a cold not only makes it difficult to breath, but it dulls your sense of taste, so that you can't even tell fresh apple pie from stale oatmeal. Illness cancels our appetite for healthy choices, and leads us to make choices that only keep us sick longer.

Moral and spiritual illness works the same way. When the inner person is languishing, we have less appetite for the good and healthy truths of God. We are unable to receive good advice from Christian friends, because our taste for spiritual truth has been dulled. We are unable to turn to the Bible for spiritual and moral nourishment, because our spiritual sense of taste, our spiritual hunger for God, has been diminished.

When our souls are sick, we need good stories—and that's why the Bible is so full of them. We need to see the truth of God brought powerfully, tangibly alive in the experience of another person who has hurt and suffered as we now hurt and suffer. When we see God's healing, loving truth in action, we experience a stirring of life and hope. When we hear the stories of God's activity in human lives, our hunger for God and His righteousness is quickened and brought to life. "I want that myself," we think. "Maybe there's hope for me."

Four scenes, four characters

There are four main characters in this story. The first three of those four characters are:

- Ruth, the Moabite woman of faith and character.
- Naomi, Ruth's grumbling, negative mother-in-law.
- Boaz, the Jewish man who falls in love with Ruth.

The romantic exchanges between Ruth and Boaz—the sexual tension of their relationship, the resolution of that tension, their marriage, and birth of their child—comprise the plot of the story of Ruth. The story of Naomi, the mother of Ruth's first husband (who died in Moab), serves as a counterpoint or subplot. Her grumbling, questioning, and struggle with God serves to contrast and underscore the beautiful faith and godliness of Ruth and Boaz.

But as I have already noted, there is a fourth character, less obvious than the first three. The fourth character is, in fact, not just one person but a collection of people:

- The townspeople.

The story takes place in Bethlehem, the city where Jesus would be born a thousand years later. In fact, the child born to Ruth and Boaz is the ancestor of David the king and the ancestor of Jesus Christ. The women of Bethlehem mentioned at the end of chapter 1, the men at the beginning of chapter 4, and the women again at the end of chapter 4 form a kind of chorus, like the chorus of an ancient Greek play. They observe what takes place, and eventually they are brought into the action of the story. As God teaches Ruth and Boaz to love each other and live lives of faith, the entire town is blessed as a result.

Four scenes make up the story—one scene in each of the four chapters of the book of Ruth. In Scene One, a father and two sons sojourn in the land of Moab during a time of famine. All three men die, and their wives are left alone. Two of the women, Naomi and one of her daughters-in-law, Ruth, decide to return to Bethlehem.

Scene Two takes place in a field at harvest. It is a scene that is richly supplied with detail and description, enabling us to use our imaginations and mentally place ourselves among these people and events. In this scene, there is a moving dialogue between Ruth and Boaz when they meet for the first time and a love relationship begins.

Scene Three takes place at night after a harvest celebration. By this time, we are becoming enchanted by the beautiful, engaging personalities of these two people, Ruth and Boaz, who are gradually falling in love with each other. In this scene, we find them lying together, whispering to each other under the stars. Though it is a chaste scene involving two people of godly, moral character, there is unmistakable sexual tension in this scene.

Scene Four takes place in the public square the following day, when Boaz declares his intention to marry Ruth. He faces a man who had prior responsibility from God to care for Ruth and Naomi, and he gives the other man the opportunity to fulfill his obligation of marriage toward Ruth. When the other man declines to do so, Boaz and Ruth are free to marry.

Each of these scenes contains a crucial conversation. From these conversations, we can learn a lot about communication, relationships, and honest emotions. We learn how to speak to one another from the heart. We learn how to connect with one another by being honest and transparent with one another about what we are truly thinking and feeling inside.

Go to any bookstore or computer-search the titles at Amazon.com on the Internet, and you will find scores of books filled with advice on romance and relationships. Let me share with you some examples of actual titles on the market. There are books that suggest that the secret to true romance is knowing how to flirt—books such as *How to Attract Anyone; Anytime, Anyplace: The Smart Guide to Flirting;* and *101 Ways to Flirt: How to Get More Dates and Meet Your Mate.*

There are books on the "rules" and "secrets" for manipulating others and maneuvering them into falling in love with you—*How to Make Anyone Fall in Love With You; The Rules: Time-Tested Secrets for Capturing the Heart of Mr. Right; 2002 Ways to Find, Attract and Keep a Mate; Guerrilla Dating Tactics: Strategies, Tips, and Secrets for Finding Romance;* and *How to Be Irresistible to the Opposite Sex.* There are books for those who are romantically inclined but not too bright, such as *Dating for Dummies* and *The Complete Idiot's Guide to Dating.*

There are books for greedy romantics, such as *How to Marry the Rich.* There are books for men, such as *A Guy's Guide to Dating: Everything You Need to Know About Love, Sex, Relationships, and Other Things Too Terrible to Contemplate.* There are books which really specialize and focus on the details, such as *The Kissing Book.* There is even a book for hardened cynics called *Love Stinks!*

Read almost any contemporary book on love and relationships or watch almost any romantic movie, and you will usually see people playing games with each other, manipulating circumstances and communication, and using various tricks, techniques, and lines on each other. But here, in this three-thousand-year-old book, we see a beautiful example of mutual honesty, mutual respect, mutual commitment, and authentic love. This story—so ancient yet so timely and contemporary—shows us what a relationship between a man and a woman *could* be and *should* be.

Familiar people, strange customs

The book of Ruth begins with these words: "Now in the days when the judges ruled, there was a famine in the land."

The book of Judges—which comes immediately before the book of Ruth—tells us of the days when the judges governed Israel. Those were among the bleakest, most cruel, most spiritually dark days in the history of the nation of Israel.

The last sentence in the book of Judges gives us an apt one-line description of the time of the judges of Israel: "In those days Israel had no king; everyone did as he saw fit"—or, as other translations put it, "Everyone did what was right in his own eyes" (Judges 21:25). In other words, each person made a god of himself. No one felt bound by the law of God, because each person devised his or her own morality, his or her own definition of spirituality.

Does that sound familiar? Don't we live in very similar times today? Today, we commonly hear people say, "You have your truth, your morality, your god, and I have mine. You can't legislate morality. No one has a right to judge my actions. I have a right to do whatever is right in my own eyes, and no one has a right to tell me I'm wrong. Morality is a private matter."

Professor Robert Simon, professor of philosophy at Hamilton College in Clinton, New York, says that today's generation of young people is different from previous generations. The present generation, whose parents were the Woodstock generation, have been raised with the belief that there should be no rules, no authority, no moral absolutes. As a result, Professor Simon sees a disturbing number of students passing through his classes who cannot bring themselves to judge *anything* as morally wrong—not even mass murder!

Writing in *U.S. News and World Report*, journalist John Leo observes that Professor Simon's experience indicates that our society is "overdosing on nonjudgmentalism" to the point where many students today do not even condemn the Holocaust—the slaughter of 6 million Jews by the Nazis during World War II. Leo notes:

In 20 years of college teaching, Prof. Robert Simon has
never met a student who denied that the Holocaust happened. What he sees quite often, though, is worse: students who acknowledge the fact of the Holocaust but
can't bring themselves to say that killing millions of people is wrong. Simon reports that 10 to 20 percent of his
students think this way. Usually they deplore what the
Nazis did, but their disapproval is expressed as a matter
of taste or personal preference, not moral judgment. "Of
course I dislike the Nazis," one student told Simon, "but
who is to say they are morally wrong?"[1]

We live in a world where the decision to slaughter one
and a half million unborn babies a year—or the decision to
slaughter six million Jews—is, to many, simply a matter of
"choice," not a matter of right and wrong. Everyone does
what is right in his or her own eyes—even though God
clearly says it is wrong. So the people and times of the story
of Ruth are people like us and times like ours, even though it
was a different culture with different customs.

Once we have noted the many *similarities* between ourselves and the people of the story of Ruth, it becomes clear
that we can identify with this story and apply its lessons to
our own lives. Then we can go on to note the interesting and
exotic *differences* between our culture and customs and those
depicted in the story of Ruth. In Ruth, we encounter a number of fascinating customs that are unfamiliar to us. The first
custom is *gleaning*, which we encounter in chapter 2. Gleaning was God's provision for the poor in Israel, and we will
take a closer look at that custom later in our study.

The second strange custom we encounter is the *levir*, the
custom of marrying a childless widow in order to maintain
the lineage of her late husband. Again, we will examine this
custom more closely at the appropriate time.

The third custom we find in Ruth is the role of the *go'el*,
the kinsman redeemer. The redeemer's role is to purchase

back for the family what has been lost under tragic circumstances. Boaz is the kinsman redeemer of the book of Ruth, and it is easy to see that he is also a metaphor of our kinsman redeemer, Jesus Christ.

There are, of course, other more subtle cultural differences between the time of Ruth and our own time, and it's important that we understand these differences so that we can properly understand the story. For example, we see that the role of women in that age was different than in ours. Women in Ruth's time did not control their own destiny. They depended on men for their security—a father, a husband, a brother, a son, or some other male figure who would care for them and preserve the family property.

It is also important to understand that the society of the time of Ruth was very much a land-based society. The Jews lived in the Promised Land given to them by God. Retaining and maintaining the family estate was critical to the identity of the Jews. In this agrarian society, a family's riches, status, and security were based entirely on the ability of the land to produce wealth.

So there are clearly differences between the time of Ruth and our own time, but these are superficial differences of culture and custom. Once you get past those surface distinctions, once you look at the hopes, dreams, feelings and relationships of the people in this story, you find that nothing has really changed. People are people, no matter what the time, no matter what the era.

Why we identify

One reason this ancient book is of such practical relevance to our lives today is that it is so easy for us to identify with the people in the story of Ruth. These are ordinary people, just like us. There is no reference in this story to people of royalty or extraordinary riches or exceptional beauty. There is nothing in this story that marks these people as so different from us that we cannot identify with them and put ourselves in their place. In many ways, we are just like them.

This is a story of human loneliness, human discovery, and human romance—feelings with which you and I are quite familiar. The story of Ruth is a storybook expression of the truth first uttered by the Lord in the creation account of Genesis: "It is not good for the man to be alone . . . ." In every age since then, God has been drawing a man and a woman together, joining them together as husband and wife, as partners and lovers for life—if they will let Him.

God's beautiful plan for humanity is that, again and again, a godly man and a godly woman will be drawn to each other, give themselves to each other in a covenant relationship before God and the human community, build a family, and raise children together in the safe, nurturing environment of a loving, God-worshipping, two-parent home. What God accomplished in the life of Ruth and Boaz some three thousand years ago, He still seeks to accomplish today, in your life, your family, and mine.

God prepared Boaz and Ruth to fit together perfectly, to complement each other, to meet each other's needs, to be precisely the right mate for each other. The dynamics of how they were brought together, how they learned to trust the will of God for their lives, how they listened to each other and to the still, small voice of God—these are the very same dynamics that we need to discover and live out in our marriage relationships today. When we follow the pattern that is set forth for us in the lives of Ruth and Boaz, we discover the same result in our own lives: the creation of a loving, lasting relationship, the banishment of aloneness, the daily delight of experiencing a deep, intimate relationship with another human being.

But the story of Ruth is more than just the story of a love between a man and a woman. It is also the story of a friendship—the very special friendship between Naomi and Ruth.

It is the story of their loyalty and commitment to each other, their willingness to take on life together, and the certainty that each of them (especially Ruth) would support the other through some of life's most difficult and trying circumstances. Some of the most tender and touching moments in the story of Ruth occur in the course of the friendship between Ruth and her sometimes difficult mother-in-law, Naomi. Together, they learn to be mutually supportive companions to one another—and they serve to instruct you and me in what it takes to be a true and honest friend to another person along life's journey.

The story of Ruth is also a story about suffering. Reading this story, we discover that human suffering hasn't changed at all in three thousand years. People today experience pain, grief, heartache, failure, loss, fear, regret, and deprivation in the very same way that people did three millennia ago. Today, just as then, God is able to use our suffering to build our faith and character. Today, just as in Ruth's time, God doesn't waste our pain; He transforms it into benefit for our lives and for His purposes. Most of all, today as then, God is with us every step of the way—not always taking us *out* of our suffering, but leading us victoriously *through* it, bringing us safely to the other side.

Risky faith in a caring God

As we walk alongside Ruth, Boaz, and Naomi, we will make the same discoveries and learn the same lessons they do. We will discover what it truly means to trust God rather than our own perception of the situation, our own human plans and purposes. We will see how it is possible to trust God's goodness and provision for our lives, even in the most desperate and even hopeless circumstances. We will learn that God is able to lead us out of the realm of spiritual darkness and despair (as He did for Ruth) or the desert of isolation (as He did for Boaz) or the wilderness of negative thoughts and attitudes (as He did for Naomi), and to transform us into people who display beautiful, godly, Christlike character.

As you journey alongside Ruth, Naomi, and Boaz, I encourage you to be alert to three themes that emerge from their story:

Theme 1: God calls us to step out in bold, risky, obedient faith. Ruth is a woman raised in Moab in a spiritually dark land dominated by a dark and false religion. She hears of the God of Israel and risks everything in order to follow Him and trust in Him. Ruth's simple, trusting faith stands in brilliant contrast to the gloomy, pragmatic attitude of Naomi, whose motto seems to be, "What you see is what you get." Ruth trusts in the promises and goodness of an unseen God; Naomi trusts only what she can see and measure. If her circumstances are pleasant, then she is happy. If life is hard and painful, then she is depressed and negative, ready to give up on life and on God.

After Ruth's husband died, Ruth's faith in God still lived. But not Naomi! True to her instincts, she said to her newly widowed daughter-in-law, Ruth, "Go back to your mother's house. Your husband has died, there is no hope for finding a husband in Israel." Ruth's reply is an expression of her faith and her godly character: "I am going with you to be with you and your God." Ruth's was a faith in the unseen, and it was so strong that she was willing to step out boldly, accepting the risks, following Naomi and the God of Israel, trusting completely and without hedging her bets.

But Ruth isn't the only person in this story who demonstrates bold, risky, obedient faith in God. The night after Ruth and Boaz lay near each other on the threshing floor and whispered to each other, Boaz risked everything—including his budding romance with Ruth—in order to be obedient to God. He approached the man who had first responsibility for Ruth and her late husband's family and land. "If you will act according to your responsibility," Boaz said in effect, "I will relinquish my hope of marrying Ruth." Trusting that God had not brought Ruth and himself together for nothing, he risked everything to call this other man to his duty according to law and tradition. As God knew would happen, the man refused. Boaz and Ruth were free to marry, according to God's law.

As you walk alongside Ruth and Boaz in this story, I believe you will be challenged by their example to a bolder, riskier, more courageous faith in your own life. I like to think of the book of Ruth as an Old Testament commentary on that great New Testament verse on faith: "We look not at the things which are seen, but at the things which are not seen; for the things which are seen are temporal, but the things which are not seen are eternal" (2 Corinthians 4:18 NASB). Ruth and Boaz bet everything—even their future together and their love for each other—on a God they could not see. They believed that an invisible God is infinitely more trustworthy and reliable than visible circumstances.

Theme 2: The hand of God is everywhere, working out His plan and our ultimate good. There is a great statement that appears in Ruth 2:3. In that chapter, we find Naomi in a mindset of frustration and bitterness. Ruth and Naomi are in poverty, and Ruth has told her mother-in-law that she is going out into the fields to glean whatever grain the field laborers had left behind (in those times, gleaning was God's way of providing for the poor). The Bible then tells us, "So she went out and began to glean in the fields behind the harvesters. As it turned out, she found herself working in a field belonging to Boaz . . ." Some translations say that Ruth "happened" to be in the field belonging to Boaz.

Now, it was no coincidence that "as it turned out" she accidentally "found herself working in a field belonging to Boaz." It didn't just "happen." It was not fate or chance or the roll of the dice that brought her there—she was steered to that field by the hand of God Himself! The providence, care, and presence of God directed and led her.

Ruth's faith in God—her absolute, simple trust in His provision and direction for her life—is doubly amazing when you consider the circumstances of her life up to this point. She has endured terrible famine and hardship in the land of Moab. Her husband has died, leaving her without security, care, and protection in the world. She has endured terrible hunger and poverty—and every twist and turn in the journey of her life seems to be leading her into even worse sorrow and deprivation.

But God is performing a magnificent work of faith in the heart of Ruth. Every difficulty, question, uncertainty, and broken heart becomes a means by which God can do even better, greater, and more amazing works through the life of Ruth. There are few things in this world more beautiful than a life that has been changed, molded, and shaped by adversity and trial into a vision of Christlikeness, as the life of Ruth has been.

Gospel singer Amy Grant tells the story of how God transformed her life. Early in her career, there was a time when she was singing all the right Christian words, but her life was a hollow, phony shell. There was enormous strife in her marriage to songwriter Gary Chapman, in large part because he was frequently strung out on cocaine. They talked about divorcing, and Amy sank into a deep depression. "For a few days, I just stayed in bed and mourned my life," she later recalled. "The only hope I could seem to see was just junking it all, moving to Europe, and starting everything all over again."

Amy's sister, seeing how distraught and depressed she was, tried to get through to Amy before she departed for Europe. "Fine," said the sister, "go to Europe, leave it all behind, start your life again. But before you go, I want you to tell my little girl how you can sing that Jesus can help her through anything in her life—but that He couldn't help you."

Those words stunned Amy Grant. She was forced to confront the fact that she was not living the message she had been singing. Over the next few days, a shaken Amy Grant turned to Jesus for hope and help. And over the weeks that followed, she and Gary were able to rebuild their lives, their faith, and their marriage—and today she sings with a new vibrancy and authenticity for God.

God often chooses to use our trials, adversity, and brokenness to bring about His healing will. It is sometimes said that "in love's service, only the wounded soldier can serve." From the life of Ruth, we learn that we must be willing to allow God to transform our weakness and pain into His power and grace for our own lives and the lives of others around us.

In Ruth 4, we see that the women of the town have reached an important conclusion. They have been listening to Naomi, observing the love of Boaz and Ruth, and examining the faith and confidence this couple demonstrated in God. They have seen Naomi holding the child born to Ruth and Boaz, and they have heard Naomi say, "The Almighty did something for me. Here is a boy who will grow to be a man who will take care of me in my old age." God had provided a male protector and provider for Naomi—and she was grateful at last.

But then the women of the town go on to make an even more profound observation: "For your daughter-in-law, who loves you and is better to you than seven sons, has given birth to him." What a powerful statement of God's guiding, providing hand! The women of the town are saying, in other words, "Look, Naomi—God was with you all along, even during all of your complaining. He provided for you in ways you didn't expect—in ways far *beyond* your meager expectations! You wanted a man to take care of you; God gave you a woman. You wanted a Jew to take care of you; God gave you a Moabite. Hasn't Ruth been better for you than seven sons would have been? Has God been absent? Has He treated you badly or unfairly? Has He failed to provide for you? No! God was there all the time—you just couldn't see Him!"

Over and over throughout the book of Ruth, we see this second theme being lived out before our eyes: The hand of God is everywhere, working out His plan and our ultimate good. He cares. He's with us. He loves us. We are always under His watchful eye, His providing hand. Even while we are taking bold steps of risky faith (risky, that is, from our limited perspective), He is always there, holding us safely in His everlasting arms.

Theme 3: God's love is all-inclusive—no one is left out. As we read the story of Ruth and Boaz, we are impressed by their faith, their courage, their sincerity, their godliness, their sweet spirits, their Christlike character. We are tempted to think, "What wonderful people! Surely God must take a special liking to such people as Ruth and Boaz." And then we look at Naomi—a real gloomy gus, the kind of person who might well be described as a "nattering nabob of negativism." We are tempted to wonder how God can stand such a person, so short on faith, on optimism, on trust in God.

But—praise God!—He doesn't judge people and lose patience with people the way we do. Even though Naomi wrestles with God throughout the story, she is loved by Him every bit as much as Ruth and Boaz are. Naomi doesn't miss out—God finds a way to win her as well!

What's more, even the townspeople of Bethlehem are won over. Though they lived in the time of the judges, in the midst of lawlessness and faithlessness, in the end they recognize and trust in God as well. These soul-sick people find that their spiritual appetite is whetted. They see that God truly can be trusted, and that living for Him in obedience is worth any risk.

So this, in a very brief overview, is the book of Ruth—a story to engage our emotions, renew our faith, and revive our hunger for God. If we read it with an open heart and an eager imagination, it is a book that will impact our relationships and change our lives. So turn the page with me. Come with me, back in time, to a distant land, a distant culture—

And discover some fascinating people who are a lot like you and me . . . .

CHAPTER 2

A TALE OF
TWO WIDOWS

Ruth 1

Charles Dickens began his classic novel, *A Tale of Two Cities*, with the now-famous lines:

> It was the best of times, it was the worst of times, it was the age of wisdom, it was the age of foolishness, it was the epoch of belief, it was the epoch of incredulity, it was the season of Light, it was the season of Darkness, it was the spring of hope, it was the winter of despair, we had everything before us, we had nothing before us, we were all going direct to Heaven, we were all going direct the other way—in short, the period was . . . like the present period . . . .

The book of Ruth could easily begin the same way. It opens with chapter 1—*A Tale of Two Widows*, Naomi and Ruth. It is the worst of times—the time of the judges, a turbulent and evil period in Israel's history, a time of famine in the land, and a time of terrible loss and grief in the lives of these two women. But as this story unfolds, we will see that it is also the best of times—a time when Ruth discovers true love, authentic love, Christlike love personified in a man named Boaz. It will also turn out to be the best of times for Naomi, as she ultimately discovers a refreshing restoration of faith in the midst of her desert of trials.

Also like Dickens' tale, the story of Ruth portrays the blossoming of wisdom in an age of foolishness; a revelation of faith in an epoch of faithlessness; a season of Light in a long night of spiritual darkness; a spring of hope against a winter of despair; a glimpse of Heaven amid hellish circumstances. And as we explore this beautiful, powerful drama together, we will see that the period and the people we find in this ancient tale are very much like the period and the people of today. Reflected in this story, we see ourselves.

The story begins with the first five verses of Ruth chapter 1:

> In the days when the judges ruled, there was a famine in the land, and a man from Bethlehem in Judah, together with his wife and two sons, went to live for a while in the country of Moab. The man's name was Elimelech, his wife's name Naomi, and the names of his two sons were Mahlon and Kilion. They were Ephrathites from Bethlehem, Judah. And they went to Moab and lived there.
>
> Now Elimelech, Naomi's husband, died, and she was left with her two sons. They married Moabite women, one named Orpah and the other Ruth. After they had lived there about ten years, both Mahlon and Kilion also died, and Naomi was left without her two sons and her husband.

The events which take place in the opening verses of Ruth cover some ten years and they are summarized very briefly by the writer of the book. In this brief summary, however, is some important and fascinating background information which will help us to understand these people and their times.

The opening phrase tells us that this story takes place during the time when the judges governed Israel, as described in the book of Judges (which comes just before Ruth in the Old Testament). One Bible commentary describes the period of the judges as characterized by "savagery, lust, strife, and lawlessness." It was one of the longest and darkest tunnels in Israel's history, when there was very little love of God or knowledge of His law.

Throughout the book of Judges, we see periods of spiritual darkness, occasionally punctuated by a moment of faith here, an act of obedience there—but those brief moments of spiritual light and hope are soon followed by yet another episode of darkness and rebellion against God. As you read through Judges, you sense a spiraling spiritual descent as events grow progressively worse, hearts grow progressively harder, sin grows progressively more pervasive. The book ends with a dismal, heart-breaking account of rape, murder, dismemberment, and genocide.

One key to understanding the time of the judges—into which the story of Ruth breaks like a ray of brilliant light!— is that there is no place in the book of Judges where anyone expresses thanks to God or appreciation for what God has done. But when we leave the book of Judges and enter the book of Ruth, we feel an immediate lift in our spirits. Here we meet two people, Ruth and Boaz, who are filled with thankfulness and acknowledgment of God.

We are also told that the time of Ruth was a time of famine. Though few of us have ever suffered through a famine, most of us are familiar with news images of famine in Asia or Africa. We have seen the haunted, desperate look on the faces of famine victims—the thin arms, the bellies swelled by malnutrition, the gaunt and hopeless faces. After all these years and all of our technological advances, famine still stalks the human race as we move into the 21st century.

And it was famine—the desperation of starvation—that stalked the land in the time of Naomi and Ruth. These events may have taken place during the time of the Midianite destruction of the southern tribes of Israel. At one point during the time of the judges, the Midianites warred against Israel, and their plunderings and pillagings did produce a famine in the land. So, in a search for food and life and security, Elimelech and his family migrated from a homeland of poverty, hunger, and despair to a strange and foreign land. This migration introduces yet another problem with which we are familiar today: the clash between cultures and nationalities.

Especially in California, where I live, we see a lot of problems as a result of illegal immigration. There are hot tempers and angry exchanges between people from different nations, different cultures, who are struggling to bridge the cultural divide and find ways to get along with one another.

Ruth was a Moabitess, while the family of Elimelech were Jews. Moab, in fact, was not only a different country than Israel, but a nation which had been at war with Israel in times past. The Moabite religious system was diametrically opposed to the worship of Yahweh (or Jehovah). Chemosh, the god of the Moabites, was a demon god who was worshipped by sacrificing and burning children in his honor. It was a dark, violent, and destructive religious system, in contrast to the light and glory that God wanted to display in his people, Israel (though the Israelite lifestyle in the time of the judges hardly displayed God's light and glory).

Another issue we see in this opening passage is the crisis of widowhood. It is tragic and painful in any place and time for a woman to lose her husband, but widowhood was particularly hard on a women during the troubled, famine-ridden time of Ruth and Naomi. There was no Social Security, no welfare system, no government "safety net," no life insurance. Women and children in Bible times needed a man to act as provider and protector—a husband, father, brother, or grown son. But Naomi had no man in her life; as verse 5 tells us, she had lost not only her husband but her grown sons as well.

Widows in the Old Testament are classic examples of utter destitution and desolation. In the Bible, the essential definition of what it means to have compassion in your heart is to care for widows and orphans—those in society who are the least powerful and the most destitute. To show compassion for widows, therefore, was the primary example in Scripture of what it means to be servant-hearted toward others.

These, then, are the times and the conditions in which this account takes place—conditions of grief, widowhood, and desolation amid a time of lawlessness, culture clash, famine, and human desperation. All the circumstances in the introductory chapter of the book of Ruth speak of hardship and despair.

The character of Naomi

The next few verses give us the human background, a sense of the real flesh-and-blood personalities in this story—and it is here, as we become acquainted with the living characters in the story of Ruth that we begin to identify, to see ourselves and the people we know. The personality of the older woman, Naomi, has a lot to do with shaping the later interaction between Ruth and Boaz. It is against the background of Naomi's personality that this loving couple's faith in God is exemplified.

In Ruth 1:6–14 we read:

> When she heard in Moab that the LORD had come to the aid of his people by providing food for them, Naomi and her daughters-in-law prepared to return home from there. With her two daughters-in-law she left the place where she had been living and set out on the road that would take them back to the land of Judah.
>
> Then Naomi said to her two daughters-in-law, "Go back, each of you, to your mother's home. May the LORD show kindness to you, as you have shown to your dead and to me. May the LORD grant that each of you will find rest in the home of another husband."

> Then she kissed them and they wept aloud and said to her, "We will go back with you to your people."
>
> But Naomi said, "Return home, my daughters. Why would you come with me? Am I going to have any more sons, who could become your husbands? Return home, my daughters; I am too old to have another husband. Even if I thought there was still hope for me—even if I had a husband tonight and then gave birth to sons—would you wait until they grew up? Would you remain unmarried for them? No, my daughters. It is more bitter for me than for you, because the LORD's hand has gone out against me!"
>
> At this they wept again. Then Orpah kissed her mother-in-law good-by, but Ruth clung to her.

This is a very touching scene. These three women—Naomi, Ruth, and Orpah—have been bonded together by their circumstances. They clearly love each other. In fact, Naomi is loved by everyone in this story. As we shall soon see, when Naomi returns to Bethlehem, the women of the town will greet her with open arms. And we will also see that Boaz, the man we will meet in Ruth chapter 2, is also very solicitous about Naomi's welfare. Throughout this story, a great number of people are consistent in their concern and love for Naomi.

This may seem odd, because we will see that Naomi is a hardened and cynical person. Why would such a person be so well-loved by the people around her? Why are people actually *drawn* to her? I believe it is because Naomi is not a one-dimensional person. She is not merely a crabby old woman. She is a complicated person, with many good, desirable qualities alongside the negative ones. I believe Naomi is a woman of great energy, great effectiveness in life. But Naomi has this flaw: she finds it very difficult to trust God when she can't see Him at work with her own eyes.

In this scene, we see a beautiful, encouraging beginning, as Naomi's two daughters-in-law tearfully express their love for her. Naomi, in turn, calls on God to bless them. But as soon as she finishes her prayer for Ruth and Orpah, she goes on to say, in effect, "I can't do anything to fix the problem. Go back to your mother's house." It is clear that Naomi doesn't expect God to act effectively in their lives; rather, she seems to believe that God needs human help in order to move circumstances.

Naomi expects no miracles, no divine intervention. She dismissively suggests one scenario: "Well, let's suppose I get married tonight. I'll find a man, marry him, and have babies. I'll do it as quickly as possible—shall you wait for these boys to grow up so you can marry them? Ridiculous! Your best bet is to go back to your mother's home, your native village, your network of friends, and find some other nice young men to marry."

I think it is significant that in the next verse, Ruth 1:15, after Orpah has left, Naomi says that Orpah has gone back to her people—and to her gods. Then, in a statement of the utter bleakness and despair of Naomi's life, she urges Ruth to do the same. But this young woman, Ruth, is very wise and loyal—loyal to her newfound God and to her mother-in-law and friend, Naomi. She knows that there is no life for her in a land of spiritual darkness.

Though Naomi trusts only what she can see and has no confidence that God will act on their behalf, though Naomi's thinking and instincts dictate that she alone can fix her circumstances, Ruth is a woman of faith. She trusts an unseen God to intervene in her circumstances. Amid hopeless circumstances, her hope is in the Lord. Beginning with verse 15, we read:

> "Look," said Naomi, "your sister-in-law is going back to her people and her gods. Go back with her."
> But Ruth replied, "Don't urge me to leave you or to turn back from you. Where you go I will go, and where

you stay I will stay. Your people will be my people and your God my God. Where you die I will die, and there I will be buried. May the LORD deal with me, be it ever so severely, if anything but death separates you and me." When Naomi realized that Ruth was determined to go with her, she stopped urging her.

So the two women went on until they came to Bethlehem. When they arrived in Bethlehem, the whole town was stirred because of them, and the women exclaimed, "Can this be Naomi?"

"Don't call me Naomi," she told them. "Call me Mara, because the Almighty has made my life very bitter. I went away full, but the LORD has brought me back empty. Why call me Naomi? The LORD has afflicted me; the Almighty has brought misfortune upon me" (15–21)

It would be easy to condemn Naomi for her cynicism—but that wouldn't be fair. Naomi was a realist. She had been hurt by life; she had suffered a great deal. She was a widow who had learned through great suffering not to trust anything that could not be tested and verified by her five senses. She did not allow fantasies, wishes, and emotions to get in the way of cold, hard facts—and she made decisions on that tough-minded, hard-headed basis.

I believe Naomi could have been a very successful businesswoman had she lived in our own era. When Orpah and Ruth call out to her emotionally—"We love each other; let's stick together and support each other through these trials"—Naomi instantly cut them off. "Don't be ridiculous!" she replies, in effect. "Let's just look at the cold, hard facts. If you go back to your parents' home, you stand a much better chance of getting a husband than if you stand by me. Whatever feelings or wishes we might have must be swept aside. To survive, we need to look at things intelligently and rationally. Get real!"

Naomi was an angry woman—she tells us so herself! Her name means "pleasant," but when she returns to Bethlehem, her home town, she insists that people call her by a new name, Mara, the Hebrew word for "bitter." She says, "My name should be 'bitter,' not 'pleasant,' because I have been dealt with bitterly." We will also see that Naomi is a manipulative woman, a schemer—and it is this angry, unresolved resentment, this *mara*-bitterness within her that fuels her manipulative behavior.

Finally, and perhaps most importantly, Naomi blames God for what has happened to her. She says so repeatedly in this passage. Verse 13: "It is more bitter for me than for you, because the LORD's hand has gone out against me!" And then, in verse 21, she adds:

> I went away full, but the LORD has brought me back empty. Why call me Naomi? The LORD has afflicted me; the Almighty has brought misfortune upon me.

Naomi is like many Christians I've known. She is not an evil woman, she is not wicked—but she is faithless. She has stopped believing that God is able to do a new thing or a good thing in her life. She has stopped believing in anything she cannot measure and account for ahead of time. Any real faith in an active, intervening, loving, powerful God has been overwhelmed by a cynical "realism," a belief that what we see is all there is and there ain't no more—no miracles, no divine provision, no divine grace.

Naomi has been hurt so badly by life that she refuses to trust God to do anything in her life or in the lives of people around her that she could not accomplish by pulling the strings herself. That is why she is so manipulative. "God won't step in and help me," she reasons, "so I'll have to help myself."

I have to say that I don't know very many people who would quickly rise above the standard set by Naomi in these verses. When we are dealt painful circumstances in life, we can usually take the first blow, and maybe even a second. But when we are pounded and pounded, again and again, by setbacks, disappointments, losses, and griefs, when our painful circumstances settle in and cause us agony that lasts day after day, year after year, most of us tend to respond as Naomi did—if not worse! We become embittered, hard, faithless. We develop a hard shell, and we retreat within it. I've seen this tendency in many Christians—and I've seen it in me.

But it needn't be so. Naomi says in verse 13, "the LORD's hand has gone out against me!" And in verse 20 and 21, she says, "The Almighty has made my life very bitter. I went away full, but the Lord has brought me back empty. . . . The Almighty has brought misfortune upon me." Naomi has drawn conclusions about life, God, and herself based on what she can see, based on her visible circumstances.

But Ruth, looking at the same circumstances, comes to a much different conclusion. Her attitude of faithfulness amid horrible circumstances is a testimony to the fact that, by God's grace, human beings have the power to choose an attitude of faith, an attitude of hope in an unseen God—even in a desert time of loss, despair, and pain.

Naomi's cynical personality becomes a backdrop for the events that are to come in this story. Her bitterness becomes the setting against which a sweet and beautiful love story will soon unfold. Like a flower blooming in an arid and desolate place, the love of Ruth and Boaz will bloom in this setting of spiritual darkness, human pain and grief, cultural strife, poverty, widowhood, and the cynical personality of Naomi.

The character of Ruth

And now, the heroine of our story. We saw an important revelation of Ruth's character in verses 15–18:

> "Look," said Naomi, "your sister-in-law is going
> back to her people and her gods. Go back with her."

But Ruth replied, "Don't urge me to leave you or to turn back from you. Where you go I will go, and where you stay I will stay. Your people will be my people and your God my God. Where you die I will die, and there I will be buried. May the LORD deal with me, be it ever so severely, if anything but death separates you and me." When Naomi realized that Ruth was determined to go with her, she stopped urging her.

Ruth's character, as exemplified here and throughout the book of Ruth, is a profound scriptural refutation of one of the most common rationalizations for sin: "I've suffered, I've been abused, I've had a hard life—and that's why I have sinned. I couldn't help turning out the way I did. With everything I've gone through I have a right to be bitter and angry—you would, too, if you went through what I did!" That is Naomi's rationalization—but it is not Ruth's.

There is a story of two brothers who were raised in the ghetto, steeped in poverty, surrounded by drugs and crime, abandoned by their father, abused by their mother, afflicted throughout childhood by misery and pain. One brother grew up to be a doctor. He worked his way through college and medical school, then he returned to the old neighborhood and gave himself to a ministry of alleviating suffering in the ghetto where he was raised. The other brother grew up to be a thief, a murderer, a drug dealer, and an addict. He ended up in prison. I'm told that a magazine reporter interviewed these two men and wrote a story comparing the very different paths their lives took. The key question the reporter asked each brother was this: "Why did you turn out the way you did?" Both brothers answered the question with the very same words: "With the childhood I had, how else could I turn out?"

One of these brothers had the attitude of Ruth. The other had the attitude of Naomi. One said, "I've suffered, I've known deprivation and tragedy and abuse, and I've dedicated my life to making sure that other children receive the love and care and attention to their needs that I never got. I've been there, and I know how ghetto kids feel. I've chosen to turn my pain into healing for them." The other said, "I've suffered, I've been abused, so I'm going to hurt others. I'm going to get even, I'm going to take what I want, I'm going to make others feel the pain I've felt. I'm going to live out my bitterness to the Nth degree."

The message of Ruth, the message of all of Scripture, is that we are not mere products of our environment and our experiences. We are not just little silver balls in a pinball machine, the course of our lives determined by the flippers and bumpers that knock us around. Our lives are not predetermined by the hurt and abuse and losses that happen to us along the way. We have the ability to make choices. We choose our actions. We choose our attitude.

Naomi chose bitterness in response to the harshness of her life. Ruth chose an attitude of love and faithfulness. How do you and I respond to the harsh and painful experiences of life? Do we rationalize an attitude of bitterness and a lifestyle of manipulation or sin? Or do we choose to respond with an attitude of love and a lifestyle of faithfulness? Do we choose the mindset of Naomi or the disposition of Ruth?

Like Naomi, Ruth was a widow, living in a foreign land without any support from her own people. She faced every dire circumstance that her mother-in-law faced, yet without bitterness and cynicism. Ruth is living proof that hard circumstances need not produce hardened spirits. We can be like Ruth. We can be sensitive, servant-hearted people even under the most difficult of circumstances.

The most vivid difference between Ruth and Naomi is the way they relate to God. Naomi blamed God and was angry with him, but Ruth demonstrated a profound gratitude for being able to know God at all. She had grown up in

Moab, taught to worship a demon as the answer to her spiritual need. She had the thankful young heart of a girl who had been raised in spiritual darkness, in a realm of evil—and then had been delivered into realms of light and joy. The attitude of Ruth could be expressed in this way: "The joy of knowing the one true, living God is so wonderful, so worthwhile, so amazing, that I can rejoice no matter what my circumstances are! Hunger and grief are temporary. The delight of knowing God is eternal!"

Moreover, Ruth exemplified a deep longing to know *more* of God. As she told Naomi, "your God [shall be] my God" (Ruth 1:16). And as we shall later see, Boaz observes Ruth's desire for God and says to her, "May you be richly rewarded by the LORD, the God of Israel, under whose wings you have come to take refuge" (Ruth 2:12). Ruth knew what it was like to live in darkness, to feel alone in an unfeeling universe, with nothing to worship but an evil, blood-thirsty demon—and that is why she eagerly sought the light of knowing God.

Most important of all, Ruth was not the kind of person who merely believed in God as Someone to pray to or as the subject of theological doctrines. Her faith in God *changed her life* and *motivated her behavior*. Her faith was active, not passive; her faith was dynamic, not static. Because of God's love in her life, Ruth naturally demonstrated a heart of love and service toward others—including those who were hard to love.

Let's face it: Naomi was not the easiest person in the world to live with. Yet it seemed natural to Ruth, having found freedom in her relationship with God, that her response should be to take the person nearest her and begin to serve her and care for her. Ruth was committed to Naomi. Her gratitude toward God produced a lifestyle of service. Her concern was not for herself but for others. Her godly love and service toward others so filled her life that she did not have time to worry and resent her own experiences.

The question naturally arises: Where did this beautiful, godly spirit of Ruth come from? The answer, I believe, has a lot to do with a choice Ruth made, a choice we can all make—a choice to live a life of *gratitude*.

The greatness of gratitude

Nationally syndicated radio personality Dr. Laura Schlessinger once received a fax from a mother in her audience. The subject of the fax was prayer and gratitude, and Dr. Laura read it on the air. The mother wrote:

> Last week, I took my children to a restaurant. My six-year-old son asked if he could say grace. As we bowed our heads, he said, "God is great, God is good, now we thank Him for our food—and I'll thank You even more, God, if Mom lets us have ice cream for dessert. Amen."
>
> Some of the other restaurant patrons nearby chuckled at the request for ice cream. But I also heard one woman remark, "That's what's wrong with this country! Kids today don't even know how to pray! Asking God for ice cream! The idea!"
>
> Hearing this, my son burst into tears and asked, "Is God mad at me?"
>
> I assured him that he had prayed a wonderful prayer, and God was very pleased. Just then, an elderly gentleman walked over, winked at my son, and said, "I happen to know that God thought that was a great prayer."
>
> "Really?" asked my son.
>
> "Cross my heart," he replied. Then, in a loud stage whisper, he pointed to the woman who had made the offending remark and said, "You know, it's too bad *she* never asks God for ice cream. A little ice cream is good for the soul." Naturally, I bought my boy ice cream for dessert that evening.
>
> Later, when the ice cream arrived, my son looked at it for a moment—then he did something I'll remember as

long as I live. Without a word, he picked up his bowl of ice cream, got up from the table, and placed the bowl on the table in front of the woman.

Smiling broadly, he told her, "Here, lady, you can have this. Ice cream is good for the soul—and my soul is good already."

Indeed, this little boy's soul *was* good already! His prayer begins with gratitude and thankfulness, and ends with a trusting faith that God is good and that He wants to give us good gifts, such as ice cream! This little boy undoubtedly taught the sour-souled woman at the next table a lot about prayer, just as Ruth had a lot to teach her sour-souled friend, Naomi, about faith in God. The beginning of faith is a heart of acknowledgment that the Lord is good, that He wants to meet our needs, and that He is the Giver of all good gifts.

What was the source of Ruth's grateful, faithful attitude? I believe that it has a lot to do with the joy she experienced when she passed from the spiritual darkness of Moab to the spiritual light of Israel. When Ruth the Moabitess married into the Jewish family of Elimelech, she made an amazing discovery—the discovery that there is one Creator-God in heaven, and that this God has made a covenant with His people. It is this God who inspires the love of humanity, giving us laws that are exalted and honorable, and which bring out the best in human beings.

I imagine that Ruth had heard the stories of the patriarchs, that she had heard the Psalms, that she had received the Ten Commandments as an inspired guide for living. Ruth knew that the great truths she had received as a result of being grafted into the Jewish family and the Jewish faith transcended all else in life—and she was grateful for the privilege of having a relationship with the God of Israel. Her connection to that truth, her lifeline to the Jewish people and the Jewish faith, was Naomi—and she had no intention of letting go of that lifeline! So Ruth said to Naomi, "Where you go I will go, and where you stay I will stay. Your people will be my people and your God my God."

In Matthew 13, Jesus compares the kingdom of God to a treasure hidden in a field and a pearl of great price. His point: When a person finds something of incalculable value, that person is willing to sell everything and do anything to possess it. That is how Ruth felt when she discovered the God of Israel, the God of her friend, Naomi. Compared with the joy and wonder of knowing Him, all else in her life meant nothing. The central facet of her statement to Naomi is this: "Your God shall be my God."

Ruth, whose perspective on life begins with a heart of gratitude, looks at life expectantly. Naomi looks at life without any expectations at all. She has been crushed in many ways, and her hope has been beaten down by the hard circumstances. But while Naomi looks at the pain of the past, Ruth looks forward to the future. While Naomi looks only at what can be seen, Ruth focuses on the unseen realities of God. While Naomi looks at the disappointment of her circumstances, Ruth looks at the joy of her hope in God. Ruth doesn't know yet what God will do, but she knows that God is good.

One of the shortest—and most important!—verses in the New Testament is 2 Corinthians 5:7, which tells us, "We live by faith, not by sight." We make our walk, our progress through life, based on faith in things we cannot see. We believe the promises of God because God Himself has given them to us. Ruth lived by faith; Naomi lived by sight. Naomi was not an evil woman, but she was very shortsighted regarding faith and the things of God. She was like the woman who criticized the little boy's ice cream prayer. That little boy, with his grateful, hopeful, expectant prayer for ice cream, had something to teach a grumpy, hard-headed woman—just a sweet, loyal, faithful Ruth had something to teach a grumpy, hard-headed woman named Naomi.

Gratitude is the reason the spirit of Ruth is such a beautiful and attractive spirit.

CHAPTER 3

TRUE FRIENDSHIP

Ruth 1

My wife, Leslie, and I have three children, and over the years, two of them have gone through very difficult medical problems. There were times that I seriously feared for my children's future. It was the most helpless, heart-wrenching feeling I've ever experienced. I'm grateful that God brought my two children through those crises.

And then I think of Naomi—a woman who lost her two sons as well as her husband. Perhaps each of them died in her arms. Living in the time of the judges, she struggled daily to survive in an era of moral chaos and national humiliation for Israel. It was a terrible time to be a Jew. Naomi's personal crisis was compounded by the fact that the land was stricken by a famine that blighted Bethlehem and the surrounding region for a period of ten years.

Naomi suffered sorrow, hunger, and incredible loss, and she was left to face life as a widow in a time that was horribly unkind to widows. Her life was filled not only with grief from the past and pain from the present, but also fear of the future. It is hard for me to imagine how much this woman must have suffered.

My heart goes out to widows like Naomi. When I stand before the congregation during Sunday morning worship, I look out and notice the widows and widowers in the congregation—people who are left alone after the loss of a lifetime partner. In many cases, I have helped to officiate at the memorial service for that lost loved one.

Naomi and her late husband, Elimelech, were probably very godly people. Elimelech's name means "my God is king" and Naomi means "pleasant." With such names, they must have come from good, godly families. Buffeted by circumstances, they moved to Moab in an attempt to survive the famine. In that land, the two sons of Naomi married Moabite daughters—and there, Elimelech and his two sons died. The sons of Naomi probably died as young men, recently married, since they left no children behind. Though the text does not reveal the cause of death, it appears that they were taken in the prime of life.

Having established these facts in the first five verses, the rest of chapter 1 is essentially a dialogue between these two women, Naomi and Ruth. These two women, speaking in two very different voices, coming from two very different perspectives and attitudes, talk about what these facts mean. To Ruth, these losses and sufferings mean something very different from what they mean to Naomi.

To understand the book of Ruth, it is important to recognize the literary device used to tell the story of Ruth. The writer of Ruth continually presents us with contrasts and parallels between Naomi and her daughter-in-law, Ruth. The circumstances that Naomi and Ruth have gone through are parallel circumstances: both are widows, both are left childless, both are poor and destitute. Moreover, Ruth lives in a foreign land as a dislocated immigrant.

But when we look at the attitudes and responses of Ruth and Naomi, the parallels end and the contrasts take shape. Ruth's response to these circumstances is completely different from Naomi's. Viewing Ruth's response side-by-side with Naomi helps us to better understand what God wants to say to us in the book of Ruth.

Life only makes sense when lived in God's presence

When bad things happen to us, it is almost inevitable that one of the first questions out of our mouths is, "Why? Why did this happen?" When catastrophe strikes, we want to understand the meaning of it. We want to place it in a context of an orderly universe under God's control. It is hard for us to accept the possibility that bad things happen for no good reason, that our suffering is meaningless and pointless. So we attempt to place our sufferings into a meaningful framework.

There are many ways we try to give meaning to the events and conditions of our lives. We see this in the story of Job, when his three friends (who have ironically become known as "Job's Comforters") sat down with him after he had suffered blow after blow, loss after loss, and told him, "You are suffering because you are guilty—there is sin in your life, and this suffering is a judgment on your sin." Many people think this way today, and inflict their judgments upon suffering people, even though the Bible makes it clear that suffering is not necessarily the result of sin.

The suffering of other people often makes us uncomfortable. If catastrophe comes into the life of a seemingly godly person, then we feel insecure: "If that godly person can be hit with such a disaster right out of the blue, then I'm not safe, either!" So we sometimes make ourselves feel safer by concluding, "He or she must have done something terrible, some hidden sin, to deserve this. If I just keep living right, that kind of suffering will never fall on me."

Some of us, when we encounter suffering, blame ourselves, thinking, "God must be punishing me for some sin I'm not even aware of—that's why I've had this financial disaster or this disease or this injury," and in the process, we pile shame and guilt onto the suffering we're already experiencing.

Some respond to suffering in life by retreating into a turtle-shell of stoicism, adopting the advice of singer Paul Simon:

> If I never loved, I never would have cried.
> I am a rock, I am an island.

This attitude responds to suffering by disengaging and retreating from life. People who adopt this response believe that if they don't let anyone get close to them, they will never be hurt. The result, of course, is that they die a long, lingering death of loneliness.

God has given us an entirely different framework in which to make sense of our suffering. It is a realistic and meaningful framework which says that if we will place our trust in Him, then we will draw meaning for all our sorrows—and all our joys—from His purposes, His reality, and His love for us. Life only makes sense when it is lived in His presence.

And *that* is what the book of Ruth is about!

The attitude of Naomi: forsaken by God

In Ruth chapter 1, we hear Naomi and Ruth speaking about the facts of their circumstances, and attempting to place those circumstances within a framework of meaning. Let's take another look at Ruth 1:6–22:

> When she heard in Moab that the LORD had come to the aid of his people by providing food for them, Naomi and her daughters-in-law prepared to return home from there. With her two daughters-in-law she left the place where she had been living and set out on the road that would take them back to the land of Judah.
>
> Then Naomi said to her two daughters-in-law, "Go back, each of you, to your mother's home. May the LORD show kindness to you, as you have shown to your dead

and to me. May the LORD grant that each of you will find rest in the home of another husband."

Then she kissed them and they wept aloud and said to her, "We will go back with you to your people."

But Naomi said, "Return home, my daughters. Why would you come with me? Am I going to have any more sons, who could become your husbands? Return home, my daughters; I am too old to have another husband. Even if I thought there was still hope for me—even if I had a husband tonight and then gave birth to sons—would you wait until they grew up? Would you remain unmarried for them? No, my daughters. It is more bitter for me than for you, because the LORD's hand has gone out against me!"

At this they wept again. Then Orpah kissed her mother-in-law good-by, but Ruth clung to her. "Look," said Naomi, "your sister-in-law is going back to her people and her gods. Go back with her."

But Ruth replied, "Don't urge me to leave you or to turn back from you. Where you go I will go, and where you stay I will stay. Your people will be my people and your God my God. Where you die I will die, and there I will be buried. May the LORD deal with me, be it ever so severely, if anything but death separates you and me." When Naomi realized that Ruth was determined to go with her, she stopped urging her.

So the two women went on until they came to Bethlehem. When they arrived in Bethlehem, the whole town was stirred because of them, and the women exclaimed, "Can this be Naomi?"

"Don't call me Naomi," she told them. "Call me Mara, because the Almighty has made my life very bitter." I went away full, but the LORD has brought me back empty. Why call me Naomi? The LORD has afflicted me; the Almighty has brought misfortune upon me."

So Naomi returned from Moab accompanied by Ruth the Moabitess, her daughter-in-law, arriving in Bethlehem as the barley harvest was beginning.

Now let's zoom in for a closer look at Naomi's attitude, and see how she tried to make sense of the suffering that had engulfed her life. We'll see her attitude in the way she prayed, gave advice to Ruth, and drew conclusions about herself.

Before we come down too hard on Naomi, we should remember that the first thing Naomi did in these circumstances was *pray*. Twice she called on God to do good to her two daughters-in-law, Ruth and Orpah. A convicting question we should ask ourselves is: "What is my first reaction in times of catastrophe, loss, or suffering? Is prayer my first response—or my last resort?"

I believe that Naomi prayed habitually. I cannot cite a verse to state that as a certain fact, but as I enter imaginatively into this story and draw inferences from her behavior, I think it is reasonable to assume that prayer was a habit in the life of Naomi. I believe that she was absolutely certain that the most profound presence in the universe was the presence of God. In Naomi's mind, nothing happened outside of His will, so He was responsible for everything that happened. He was powerful enough to do whatever He chose. If that was true, only a fool would choose *not* to pray! So we should commend Naomi for taking God seriously.

Verse 6 contains an interesting statement: "When she heard in Moab that the LORD had come to the aid of his people by providing food for them, Naomi and her daughters-in-law prepared to return home from there." It doesn't say that Naomi heard that the rains had come back, or that meteorological conditions were now favorable. *She heard that God had come to His people.* The reason there was no more famine was that God had acted.

So Naomi concluded that God was kind—sometimes. In verse 8, she said to Ruth and Orpah, "May the LORD show kindness to you . . . ." So even though Naomi didn't trust in God's kindness, she figured it was at least worth praying for.

Naomi's attitude seems to be one of, "Don't expect anything, and you won't be disappointed—but hey, it never hurts to ask!"

A woman whose first comment in this dire crisis was about her prayer life must have prayed and prayed during those ten years. She must have prayed that the famine would soon be over, and that they could go back to their home. And when her husband became sick, she must have prayed fervently for his healing. And when her first son got sick, she certainly must have poured out her heart in prayer. Then, when her second son got sick, she must have begged God to spare her only remaining son. After burying her husband and her two children, she must have asked God for relief from all these losses, all this suffering. Again and again, Naomi prayed—and again and again, God's answer to her, delivered in the form of disappointing circumstances, was "No."

Yet Naomi did not stop praying.

It's significant that Naomi said to her two young daughters-in-law, "May the LORD deal kindly with *you*" (NASB). She did not say, "May the LORD deal kindly with *us*." She had stopped praying for herself. She had concluded that God hated her. In her mind, it was God's prerogative to hate whom He chose to hate. So Naomi stopped asking favors from God. To her, God's power was certain, but His love was fickle, selective, and undependable.

In this passage, we also see that Naomi gives advice to Ruth, and her advice is an interesting revelation of her perspective on reality and the character of God. She comes across as a sarcastic pragmatist. Her reasoning seems to go like this: Only a fool would choose not to pray, but once you're done praying, you have to live as if you can count on nobody but yourself. You have to face the facts as they are, calculate the possibilities, maximize the opportunities for yourself. God may help or He may not—but once you've prayed, the prudent thing is to simply leave Him out of the equation.

Naomi's daughters-in-law make an important statement in verse 10: "We will go back with you to your people." Naomi's people were the Jews, the covenant people of God, the ones who received the promises and the Law, the ones God had chosen to work through in a special way throughout history. These two women wanted to join the community of those who knew the Lord.

But Naomi replies, in effect, "Don't be a fool. Who's going to marry a woman of Moab in Israel in the time of the judges, when everybody is selfish and lawless? You have no hope of getting a husband if you come back to Israel with me. Return to your own homes. At least you'll have a chance of surviving and finding a husband there." Then she adds a sarcastic statement that even if she weren't too old, and could raise up sons again for them to marry, they would have no hope. In effect, she ridicules their expression of loyalty, making the entire idea of staying with her seem silly, and making it clear that their loyalty is misplaced. "God doesn't help me, so there's nothing I can do to help you," she tells them. "Go home and help yourselves."

In verse 15, when Naomi finds she cannot persuade Ruth to leave, she says, "[Orpah] has gone back to . . . her gods." That is one of the most heart-breaking statements in the entire Bible. Orpah had originally stood shoulder-to-shoulder with Ruth in her loyalty to Naomi—but Naomi's harsh, pragmatic, sarcastic assessment apparently convinced this young woman to return to Moab and to the worship of the demon-god, Chemosh. The Moabites worshipped an image of him that featured an open mouth with fire inside. Living children were tossed into the open mouth to perish in the flames. That is the god Naomi sent Orpah back to—and Ruth as well!

It's heart-wrenching to realize how little hope Naomi had. After years of praying to God, of being bitterly disappointed, of burying a husband and two sons, Naomi was willing to send Orpah and Ruth back into spiritual darkness, a land that was just one step away from the brink of hell.

Finally, we have two statements of Naomi's convictions about herself. In verse 13 she says, "It is more bitter for me than for you, because the LORD's hand has gone out against me!" Naomi has sunk into deep self-pity and bitterness—and it's not hard to understand why she has concluded that God has it in for her.

In verse 20, she returns to the town of Bethlehem, and when the people come out to greet her, she changes her name. "Don't call me Naomi [pleasant] anymore. There's nothing pleasant about me. Call me wretched, bitter, angry. God has dealt bitterly with me. I went out full, and I've come back empty." In her mind, she had woven the facts of her losses, sufferings, and pain into a bleak, dark tapestry of despair and hopelessness. Naomi believed in God, but her God was unreliable and had mistreated her. This, in Naomi's embittered mind, was "reality." This was her "truth."

Dr. Ray Stedman used to tell the story of an old woman and a preacher. She would come up and list all her problems in life at the end of every service, and he would try to give her some positive reason to look at life more optimistically. Her response to the preacher was, "You know, young man, when God sends tribulations, He expects you to tribulate." Well, Naomi knew how to tribulate—and then some! She had gone beyond merely tribulating amidst her tribulations. She had decided that God didn't love her. He loved some people, but not her.

That was Naomi's conclusion—but was she right about God? Or was she mistaken? Did Naomi truly come back empty? Was she alone when she returned to Bethlehem?

No, there was a young woman with her. In Naomi's pain-distorted, bitterness-skewed perspective, Naomi was alone. But from God's perspective, Naomi returned to Bethlehem with the whole future of the human race holding onto her arm! She came back with Ruth the Moabitess, a young woman who would be the mother of Obed, the father of Jesse, the father of David the king of Israel—the father of the Messiah of Israel, the Lord of the nations, the Lamb of God who would take away the sins of the world. Naomi was not empty—she was, in fact, more full, more rich, more blessed than she could ever imagine.

Yet in her bitterness she couldn't see it. The facts of her existence became a distorted world-view, reality-view, and God-view in her mind: "I'm empty, I'm nothing, I'm God-forsaken."

The attitude of Ruth: gratitude toward God

The world-view and God-view of Naomi contrasts vividly with Ruth's declaration of the truth. It's interesting that Ruth never says, "Naomi, I'm going to go back with you to Bethlehem because God will surely provide a husband for me there." She listened patiently while Naomi listed all the reasons why Ruth should leave and return to Moab, why Ruth had no hope of finding a husband or security in life—and Ruth didn't argue with her. In fact, she tacitly agreed with everything Naomi said. There was no evidence that Ruth believed she would ever have a husband again.

One of the interesting interpretive issues that arise in the first five verses of chapter 1 is the question of how soon in the ten-year period Ruth and her husband were married. If it was early on, and she had lived for some years with a husband and had not had a child, there may have been some question in her mind as to whether she would ever be able to have children. And she would certainly be no prize catch in Israel for several other reasons: She wasn't a Jew. She had no money or property. She had nothing to offer a prospective husband in Israel—so why would anyone want to marry her?

But Ruth refuses to accept Naomi's cynical "bottom-line" analysis of her future. Ruth responds with beautiful optimism and trust in the goodness of the Lord: "Don't urge me to leave you or to turn back from you. Where you go I will go, and where you stay I will stay. Your people will be my people and your God my God. Where you die I will die, and there I will be buried. May the LORD deal with me, be it ever so severely, if anything but death separates you and me," she says in verses 16 and 17. In other words, "God has given us each other, so let's stick together."

Naomi didn't believe that human love had much value in a cold, cruel world. But Ruth believed their love had value—and in fact was all the more valuable amid bleak and painful circumstances. Despite her cynicism and bitterness, there must have been something about Naomi that inspired love and affection in people. Ruth clearly loved her. Orpah cried when Naomi sent her away, so Orpah must have loved her. And when Naomi came back to the town of Bethlehem, all the people of the town rushed out to see her.

Yes, there was definitely something attractive about Naomi. She was charismatic and energetic, and she probably overshadowed her husband when he was alive. She was one of those people who fought life, who wrestled with God, who wanted the best, who had a deep heart and a deep love for people, and they loved her back. The tragedy of Naomi's life was that, while she had so much to offer, so much that inspired love and affection in others, she had given up her trust in the Lord.

But even though Naomi had given up on God, Ruth refused to give up on Naomi. "You know," Ruth told Naomi, "I may never have anyone but you. But you're enough for me. The relationship God has given us as mother and daughter, as friends, as companions in suffering, is enough for me. God has not been bad to us—He's been good to us in ways we didn't expect. So don't send me away. Where you go, I will go. Where you lodge, I will lodge. Your people will be my people. Your God will be my God. Where you die, I will die and be buried."

The difference between Naomi and Ruth can be reduced to a single word: *gratitude*. Naomi chose to focus on what she had lost. Though Ruth had lost much herself, she chose to focus on what she had gained. Naomi chose to focus on God's seeming refusal to answer her prayers. Though Ruth had undoubtedly received the same answer to her own prayers, she chose to focus on the fact that she no longer prayed to a fiery, child-consuming demon, but to the God of Israel, the God of the universe.

Ruth had come out from among a people with no future but darkness, terror, and hell. She had joined the people of God, the heirs of the promise, the ones to whom the Law had been given, the ones from whom Messiah would come. She had once been a stranger to God. Now she walked in true intimacy with God. She had lost her husband, and that was a painful reality—but she had gained a friend in Naomi. Happily, her analysis of life, God, and reality was 180 degrees out of phase with Naomi's assessment.

Ruth's statement in verse 16 is often used in wedding services: "Where you go I will go, and where you stay I will stay. Your people will be my people and your God my God." This is a misapplication of that statement, since it is made not between a husband and wife, but between two close friends, two women, a mother-in-law and a daughter-in-law. I don't suppose it does any real harm to use these words in a wedding service—they are valid words in a marriage context as well.

But it is unfortunate that so many people hear these words without realizing where they came from, who originally spoke them, and under what circumstances. It is strategically important that we, as Christians, understand that the depth of commitment expressed in these words is exchanged not between lovers, but between friends, between what we would call in a Christian context "sisters in Christ." We, in the church of Jesus Christ, should be expressing this same depth of commitment to one another on a regular basis. The church should be demonstrating to the world that it is possible to have non-sexual, non-romantic relationships of tremendous depth, absolute commitment, and authentic Christlike love. In a world where people despair of ever knowing what a truly healthy, committed relationship or friendship is all about, we must send a message: In Christ, you can know a depth of relationship, belonging, and caring you have never even imagined before!

In our rootless, mobile, transient society, relationships have become unstable and disposable. Neighborhoods and workplaces are in constant flux. For the vast majority of people, especially in urban settings, no one stays the same, no one knows their neighbors, and the workplace has become an arena of cut-throat competition. There are few possibilities for commitments to blossom and grow deep. Because sexuality produces intense emotions and a momentary sense of deep connection with another human being, people today often substitute sex for genuine relationships. Some become involved in serial love affairs or serial marriages. Others openly advocate adultery as "healthy" and "normal." Some sanction gay marriages or domestic partners.

Tragically, most people in our society see only one way of deeply connecting with another human being: sexual/ romantic attraction. If the church does not speak out with the voice of Ruth, proclaiming a depth of commitment and relationship rooted in Christlike love instead of sexuality, the world will completely miss out on the best relationships human beings can ever know.

Here in the book of Ruth is a relationship of extraordinary commitment—a relationship that has a future, substance, and authentic love. There are many people today who need to hear this message—people who for one reason or another, in one way or another, find themselves in circumstances very much like the circumstances of Ruth. They long for a depth of friendship and companionship, even though they do not expect to ever marry. Or perhaps they struggle with their sexual identity and same-gender attractions. Or perhaps they have elderly parents who require all their time and attention, so that they have no time for a romantic life. Or perhaps they have emotional quirks in their personality that make it hard for them to be committed or to attract a mate. For whatever reason, there are some people who don't expect to marry.

It would be fascinating to read the diary of one such person who has learned the lesson of the story of Ruth, and who has applied that lesson to his or her own life, even if they never expect to marry. I believe such a person would write, "By the grace of God, I have a family. I don't have a mate, I don't have a romantic attachment, but praise God! I have brothers and sisters who love me and who are involved in my life. They care about me, and I care about them. I have a place to belong. I do not live alone."

I think the dazzling beauty of the love story that unfolds in Ruth chapter 2 sometimes blinds us to the equally beautiful non-sexual, non-romantic love story in Ruth chapter 1. Here, in the friendship between Naomi and Ruth, we see a relationship that is utterly committed, honest, pure, and true—and the tragedy of Naomi's life is that she doesn't even realize it!

Naomi is frustrated, angry, and bitter because she has decided that God doesn't love her. Ruth, who has been dealt much the same hand in life, comes to a different conclusion. The first chapter of Ruth presents us with a choice: Will we approach our own lives, our own circumstances, our own trials and losses with the bitter attitude of Naomi—or the sweet spirit of Ruth?

If you are a Christian, then you are a child of God. Your body is the residence of the Holy Spirit. You have the option of being thankful, of leaning into the future, holding onto what is good—or you can conclude with Naomi that a painful past means that God is against you.

Facts are facts, and wishing can't change them. We can't wish away an abusive childhood, or the death of a spouse, or the loss of a career, or the dissolution of a dream, or the rejection of a loved one, or a diagnosis of cancer. But while facts can't be changed, the way we respond to those facts, and the way we arrange those facts into a view of God and reality, *can* be changed. We can choose a world-view of bitterness—or a world-view of gratitude. The choice is ours alone to make.

The good news of the book of Ruth is that God doesn't leave Naomi in her bitterness. When people are frustrated and angry, and they pray with their fists clenched at God, when they scream and struggle against life, God doesn't toss them aside. In fact, when you read the stories of people such as Jacob and Job and Naomi and Peter and Paul, you almost get the feeling that God has a special place in His heart for such people! As we shall see, Naomi is going to be changed—but not without a struggle.

You and I can be changed, too. We don't have to live like Naomi—dragged kicking and screaming into a trusting relationship with God. We can live like Ruth, freely and voluntarily surrendering each day as an act of gratitude and worship to God.

The plot prepares to thicken

The first chapter of Ruth ends with a glimmering of hope—the plot of this romance story is about to thicken. And as usual, in any good story, the thickening of the plot takes place with the introduction of a new, significant character. In the last verse of Ruth 1 we read:

> So Naomi returned from Moab accompanied by Ruth the Moabitess, her daughter-in-law, arriving in Bethlehem as the barley harvest was beginning.

As the barley harvest gets underway in the sleepy little town of Bethlehem, this tale of two women is about to become a completely new and fascinating tale—the story of a man and a woman. Boaz is waiting in the wings, about to step onto the stage of our story—

Stay tuned!

CHAPTER 4

A Man and
A Woman

Ruth 2

I once came across a newspaper story that arrested my attention, and which I have reproduced below. Though I have changed the name of the man in the story, all other details are as they appeared in the newspaper article:

> John Doe wants to begin life again at 50 with a new wife who will bear him six children. He has placed a display advertisement in the *Palo Alto Times*, scheduled to begin running next week, listing his qualifications.
>
> Doe's requirements for the ideal wife are: "Age— between 22 and 35; slim athletic body; able to play tennis, golf, jog and dance; must be a Christian who loves children; must be a non-smoker and nondrinker, and a person vitally into good nutrition."
>
> Doe will include his telephone number in the advertisement so that wife candidates can phone him, noting that, "We can talk it over and they will know what I am searching for." Likely choices will be invited for a personal interview at his home.
>
> Doe declared that the woman's "sweetness" will be the determining factor in whether he selects her, although, of course, she must meet the other criteria.

I ask you: Does this sound like a wise or Christian way to find your life's mate? A classified ad, interviewing "candidates," measuring each one by a set of nit-picky "criteria"? Somehow, I have to believe that God has a rather different plan for bringing a man and a woman together. We begin to catch a glimpse of that plan in the opening verses of Ruth chapter 2.

The entire second chapter of Ruth is amazing for a couple of reasons. One reason is the wealth of detail it contains. Contrast this passage with the opening section of Ruth 1, which telescopes ten years of events into a mere five verses. In Ruth 2, we have a richly detailed narrative which even includes such dialogue as the biblical version of "Good morning!" ("The LORD be with you!" "The LORD bless you!") The writer of the book of Ruth was a magnificent storyteller, with a strong narrative sense. He knows when to move his story along quickly and when to linger on details of emotion, conversation, and description.

Though ten years whiz by in the first five verses of Ruth 1, chapter 2 zooms in for a close-up view of a single twenty-four hour period. In Ruth 1:1–5, a famine begins and ends, a family migrates, two marriages take place, and three men die. But Ruth 2 focuses our attention on feelings, conversations, and intimate details, and this fact ought to persuade us to listen very carefully to the details, to observe the scene, to imaginatively enter into the feelings these people experience. For three thousand years, people have been blessed and transformed by paying careful attention to the events that take place as Ruth and Boaz begin their relationship.

The second amazing facet of Ruth chapter 2 is its spontaneity. None of the events in this chapter are planned or pre-arranged by anyone. There is not a single conversation or decision to go someplace that is part of anyone's scheme to orchestrate events. No one even anticipates what is about to happen. Everything you see and hear in this narrative is simply the result of people who faithfully live out their lives. As in the slogan of the *Candid Camera* TV show, the people in Ruth chapter 2 are simply "caught in the act of being themselves"—and in the process of being caught off-guard, they reveal their inner character.

The character of Boaz

As Ruth 2 opens, Naomi and Ruth have returned from the land of Moab and have entered Bethlehem just as the barley harvest begins. At this point, we are introduced to the third central character of this story, the man named Boaz. In Ruth 2:1–16 we read:

> Now Naomi had a relative on her husband's side, from the clan of Elimelech, a man of standing, whose name was Boaz.
>
> And Ruth the Moabitess said to Naomi, "Let me go to the fields and pick up the leftover grain behind anyone in whose eyes I find favor."
>
> Naomi said to her, "Go ahead, my daughter." So she went out and began to glean in the fields behind the harvesters. As it turned out, she found herself working in a field belonging to Boaz, who was from the clan of Elimelech.
>
> Just then Boaz arrived from Bethlehem and greeted the harvesters, "The LORD be with you!"
>
> "The LORD bless you!" they called back.
>
> Boaz asked the foreman of his harvesters, "Whose young woman is that?"
>
> The foreman replied, "She is the Moabitess who came back from Moab with Naomi. She said, 'Please let me glean and gather among the sheaves behind the harvesters.' She went into the field and has worked steadily from morning till now, except for a short rest in the shelter."
>
> So Boaz said to Ruth, "My daughter, listen to me. Don't go and glean in another field and don't go away from here. Stay here with my servant girls. Watch the

field where the men are harvesting, and follow along after the girls. I have told the men not to touch you. And whenever you are thirsty, go and get a drink from the water jars the men have filled."

At this, she bowed down with her face to the ground. She exclaimed, "Why have I found such favor in your eyes that you notice me—a foreigner?"

Boaz replied, "I've been told all about what you have done for your mother-in-law since the death of your husband—how you left your father and mother and your homeland and came to live with a people you did not know before. May the LORD repay you for what you have done. May you be richly rewarded by the LORD, the God of Israel, under whose wings you have come to take refuge."

"May I continue to find favor in your eyes, my lord," she said. "You have given me comfort and have spoken kindly to your servant—though I do not have the standing of one of your servant girls."

At mealtime Boaz said to her, "Come over here. Have some bread and dip it in the wine vinegar."

When she sat down with the harvesters, he offered her some roasted grain. She ate all she wanted and had some left over. As she got up to glean, Boaz gave orders to his men, "Even if she gathers among the sheaves, don't embarrass her. Rather, pull out some stalks for her from the bundles and leave them for her to pick up, and don't rebuke her."

So Ruth gleaned in the field until evening. Then she threshed the barley she had gathered, and it amounted to about an ephah. She carried it back to town, and her mother-in-law saw how much she had gathered. Ruth also brought out and gave her what she had left over after she had eaten enough.

Her mother-in-law asked her, "Where did you glean today? Where did you work? Blessed be the man who took notice of you!"

Then Ruth told her mother-in-law about the one at whose place she had been working. "The name of the man I worked with today is Boaz," she said.

"The LORD bless him!" Naomi said to her daughter-in-law. "He has not stopped showing his kindness to the living and the dead." She added, "That man is our close relative; he is one of our kinsman-redeemers."

Then Ruth the Moabitess said, "He even said to me, 'Stay with my workers until they finish harvesting all my grain.' "

Naomi said to Ruth her daughter-in-law, "It will be good for you, my daughter, to go with his girls, because in someone else's field you might be harmed."

So Ruth stayed close to the servant girls of Boaz to glean until the barley and wheat harvests were finished. And she lived with her mother-in-law.

Gleaning was God's welfare program, a provision of God's law to protect poor people from devastation. A landowner was not permitted to reap his field all the way to the border of his property; he had to leave a measure of unharvested grain or fruit around the edge so the poor could come and retrieve a bit of produce. During the harvest, if the reapers dropped grain on the ground, they weren't allowed to pick it up. They had to leave it so the poor could come and gather it to sustain themselves.

This is what Ruth asked her mother-in-law to be allowed to do. She awoke one morning and said to Naomi, "Let me go glean." Naomi, who is grumping and harrumphing her way through life, is not inclined to go glean for herself. It may be that she is too old—or perhaps she is simply too proud. But Ruth, with typical optimism, says, "If we are poor and God has made provision for the poor, let's go through the door the Lord has opened. It's the only one we have."

So Ruth starts early in the morning and works hard all day. She is taking the outstretched hand that God offered. It isn't much—and certainly not enough to make Ruth Naomi prosperous, but it will at least keep them alive another day.

In contrast to Ruth and Naomi—two poverty-stricken widows—Boaz is a man of means, a man of property and wealth, a businessman who employs others to work for him. We are struck by the way he relates to his subordinates, to the "little people" in his life. When he came to the field, his first act was not to take inventory or bark orders. His first act was to bless his workers, and he received a blessing in return. He cared about the well-being of the people around him—including their spiritual well-being. He loved God and he wanted others to love God and receive God's blessings.

Boaz was sufficiently well-acquainted with his workers that he recognized a newcomer among them, gleaning in the field. A selfish businessman would not have noticed the gleaners; he might even resent them as intruders on his property. But Boaz, though wealthy, was not greedy, nor was he an exploiter of his workers. He cared enough about people that he noticed them and took a personal interest in them.

Whenever I read this passage, I am rebuked. I am forced to ask myself, "What kind of man am I? How do I treat the servant people, the 'little people,' the workers and subordinates in my life? How do I treat waitresses and gas station attendants and grocery clerks and gardeners whose job it is to take care of me and make my life easier? Do I care about them and their needs? Do I long for God's best in their life? Do I bless them? Do I even notice if changes have taken place in their lives?"

Boaz noticed such things. He was a boss, but he was never bossy. He was an authority figure, but he was never authoritarian. He was wealthy, but he never lorded it over on people. He cared about his workers, and in return his workers were responsive and respectful to him. This should come as no surprise. A man who cares about the people who work for him is probably going to have people who are enthusiastic and motivated about what they do. (This is a sound, biblical principle of business management!)

Ruth and Boaz meet

How did Ruth and Boaz meet? Ruth 2:3 tells us, "As it turned out, she found herself working in a field belonging to Boaz, who was from the clan of Elimelech." This was a large field that was divided into sections. Ruth walked out of town and unwittingly picked the section of the field that belonged to Boaz. She was there because she wanted to glean so that Naomi would have something to eat. She had no other motive for being in that field.

Boaz was there because he cared about his workers, and he noticed Ruth because he cared about the gleaners. Neither Ruth nor Boaz had any thoughts of romance or finding "Mr. Right" or "Miss Right" at that moment. From a human perspective, Ruth and Boaz seem to be brought together by pure coincidence—but the more important perspective is *God's* perspective. From a divine perspective, we can see that Ruth and Boaz were brought together precisely because they were thinking not of themselves but of others. Ruth was there because of her servant attitude toward Naomi. Boaz was there because of his servant attitude toward his workers. God was able to arrange the circumstances for their meeting *because both Ruth and Boaz had a heart for others*!

There is an important principle embedded in this story: The less concerned we are about our own needs, and the more committed we are to serving others, the more we allow God to arrange events and circumstances for our ultimate good. God is free to arrange things so that we can interact with people and discover truth and encounter wonderful experiences if we are not worried about ourselves, if we are not "looking out for Number One."

And there is yet another important principle in this story: We never know in life what might be truly important in our lives. Sometimes life turns on a dime. "Minor" events often have magnified consequences—and we may not see how important those "minor" events truly were until months or years later.

It has been said that life must be lived forward but can only be understood backwards. In other words, we can only live life a day at a time—but months or years later, we can see how God was able to use seemingly inconsequential "chance" occurrences in our lives to move our lives in a dramatic and powerful way. A "chance" conversation on a street corner may lead to a totally new career. You might "just happen" to see a newspaper ad which leads you to a new home in which to raise your family and build lasting memories. A "chance" encounter with an old school friend may give you a chance to lead that person to Christ.

These "chance happenings" are not accidents at all—they are God's deliberately engineered twists of heavenly serendipity. When our hearts are tuned to His heart, when our spirits are aligned with His Spirit, when our love is patterned after his, He is able to arrange all these wonderful surprises in our lives. Our job as Christians is to be sensitive to those around us and open-hearted to God.

From a purely human perspective, Boaz himself appears to be an extraordinary coincidence. It is amazing that such a man should even exist! We know little about his prior history, and we have to guess at a number of aspects of this man's background and personality, but I think we can make some reasonable guesses.

For example, it is unthinkable in that ancient culture that a man of his age (for, as we will later see, Boaz describes himself as an old man) could be a wealthy landowner, an elderly squire, without ever being married. Our best guess is that Boaz was probably married before, and his wife is now dead. It is clear, as the story unfolds, that he is not married now, and that he either has no children or (more likely) his children have grown up, received their inheritance, and moved away to start their own families.

Another amazing fact about Boaz: Naomi is initially unaware that Boaz—a man who is in the position of kinsman-redeemer to her and to Ruth—is single and available as a candidate for marriage. If she had been aware that Boaz and Ruth could marry, she undoubtedly would have been hard at work, trying to do a little matchmaking. Instead, she is slumped in despair while Ruth decides to go glean in the fields. It doesn't occur to Naomi to say, "Good idea! Go glean in the field of my rich, available kinsman Boaz!" So when Ruth goes gleaning, she doesn't know who he is. She just happens onto his field—the first field she comes to.

Another amazing fact about Boaz: He is a caring, sensitive man. He blesses his workers and cares about their welfare. He takes notice of Ruth, a stranger in his field. He shows a genuine interest in the people around him. This man of wealth and influence and power displays character that is rare among men of wealth and influence and power: He uses his position and power to help others, not to lord it over others or exploit others. That is a rare capacity in a powerful man, whether in ancient times or today, and I am always profoundly encouraged and inspired when I see influential men today who use their position and their power in Boaz-like ways to serve God and others.

Here we see a confluence of unexpected and amazing factors, all converging in the person of this man, Boaz. It is very unlikely that Ruth should just happen to stumble onto the property of a man who is kind, compassionate, wealthy, powerful, unmarried, lonely and in need of companionship, and in the unique position of kinsman-redeemer to Naomi. Such "coincidences" do not happen by mere chance. They happen only in the loving, thoughtful, carefully-laid plans of God.

A godly man and a godly woman

Notice the conversation that takes place between these two people. Boaz and Ruth display an incredible natural ability to be a man and a woman, to be what God made them to be. The day they meet, each of them has independently experienced a number of years of a deep love relationship with God. Each has a spirit that we instantly recognize as Christlike. Each of them has the serene assurance that the Lord God will meet their needs. As a result, they have a natural ability to relate to each other as a godly man and a godly woman.

Boaz initiates the relationship by serving Ruth's needs. In front of his workers and everybody else, he honors her. He says to this poverty-stricken woman, this poor gleaner, this nobody, "I have heard that you are a godly woman." He insists that she should get enough to eat and that she should sit where the workers sit. He himself serves her roasted grain. He tells his workers to pull grain stalks out of the sheaves and throw them down so that rather than just gleaning what is in the dirt, Ruth will come away with an abundance of food. He insists that she be protected, because gleaning could be a hazardous business, leaving a poor and powerless woman at risk for robbery, violence, or rape.

Boaz says to Ruth, in effect, "Let me care for you. Let me make sure you have enough to drink. It's hot out here, so I want you to drink from the same water my own workers draw. I don't want you to glean as a poor person with no other provision. I want to honor you, provide for you, and protect you." He goes on to speak of God's provision: "May the LORD repay you for what you have done. May you be richly rewarded by the LORD, the God of Israel, under whose wings you have come to take refuge." In other words, "The God from whom you have sought help is going to care for you."

Ruth is astonished by the personal, caring interest Boaz takes in her. She responds, in effect, "Why would you even look at me, since I'm a foreigner? I have no standing, no claim on your attention. Why would you care about me?"

There's a wonderful intimacy about the interchange between them. Each is delighted with the other, each is surprised. Each expresses feelings spontaneously—and it is clear that they have developed a tender relationship in a very short period of time. Ruth, who already approaches life with a deep sense of gratitude to God, finds it very easy to express gratitude to Boaz—and Boaz is intensely attracted to her beautiful spirit.

We see the provision of God behind all this. While Naomi stays at home, assuming the worst, believing that God has it in for her, Ruth always assumes the best. Her heart is full of love for God, so the Lord is able to steer her into greater and greater opportunities, greater and greater blessings. Ruth is not surprised that God is meeting her needs, because her life has been transformed by the knowledge of His love and provision for her life. If He loved her enough to move her from the darkness of Moab to the light of Israel, He would continue to love her, sustain her, and bless her. In Ruth's mind, this was only natural. Ruth's trusting, grateful attitude was the source of her life of faith.

At the same time, it seems only natural to Boaz that he should initiate a relationship with Ruth, that he should honor her and serve her needs, that he should provide for her and protect her. And Ruth is grateful to Boaz. She never intended or expected to win his favor, but in a very feminine and beautiful way she expresses her gratitude to him. From my own experience, I think I know how Boaz must have felt at that moment. As a man, I know how good it feels to receive expressions of gratitude and appreciation from my wife. That is a feminine behavior which I readily respond to, and it was a very natural, unfeigned behavior on Ruth's part. She did not have to work at it or fake it. Gratitude was in her character—and Boaz was charmed by that aspect of her character. In Ruth 2:13, we read:

"May I continue to find favor in your eyes, my lord," she said. "You have given me comfort and have spoken kindly to your servant—though I do not have the standing of one of your servant girls."

This is a very powerful expression of thanks and humility, and Ruth's attitude reaches right to the soft core of Boaz's male heart. As a result, there is an ease and grace at the very beginning of this relationship that we all find entrancing and attractive.

As I study Scripture, I am increasingly convinced that being a real man or a real woman is not very difficult. There is not much to it—it comes naturally. But if today's men and women ever discovered that fact, it might cause the economy to crash! There are entire industries built on books, magazines, seminars, and TV shows about "how to be a real man" or "how to be a real woman." Billions of dollars are spent in these areas every year—needlessly.

Being a real man or a real woman is not brain surgery, it is not rocket science; it is a simple matter of being the kind of man, the kind of woman, God intended us to be. When we look at the example of Boaz and Ruth, we see something take place that is very easy, graceful, unplanned, and simple. It is not a matter of technique or manipulation at all. It is just a matter of being a godly human being.

Now, I'm not saying it is easy to be godly. It is not easy to be selfless, faithful, loving, compassionate, and focused on others instead of self. Our selfish will gets in the way, and that makes it hard—hard, but not complicated. Becoming people like Ruth and Boaz, people who are servant-hearted and grateful, humble and thankful, is not an easy matter—but it is very uncomplicated. Once we have made the difficult choice to become uncomplicated, loving, Christlike people, then *real* masculinity and *real* femininity in relationships becomes very easy.

The Scripture says that we, as men and women, are fellow heirs of the grace of life. In Christ, there is "neither . . . male nor female, for you are all one in Christ Jesus. If you belong to Christ, then you are . . . heirs according to the promise" (Galatians 3:28–29). So men and women belong together. We belong in a kind of mutual aid and growth together, though we are often sidetracked by sin. If we deny sin by our faith in Christ, we will find ourselves, as real men and real women, supportive of each other, respectful toward each other, and compassionate toward each other's needs.

Already, we can see that this first section of the story of Ruth contains profoundly relevant lessons that we can apply to our own lives: We see that circumstances do not have to determine our response and our behavior in life. Regardless of circumstances, we have the power to choose our attitude and our actions. We see that when we choose to become godly people with a godly attitude, we allow God to arrange the circumstances of our lives in a way that brings honor to Him and benefit to us. And we have seen that when we live with an attitude of humility, thankfulness, and servant-heartedness toward others, we fully become what God created us to be: *real* men and *real* women of God.

Romance among the sheaves

We see the flowering of the love-relationship between Ruth and Boaz in verses 14–16:

> At mealtime Boaz said to her, "Come over here. Have some bread and dip it in the wine vinegar."
> When she sat down with the harvesters, he offered her some roasted grain. She ate all she wanted and had some left over. As she got up to glean, Boaz gave orders to his men, "Even if she gathers among the sheaves, don't embarrass her. Rather, pull out some stalks for her from the bundles and leave them for her to pick up, and don't rebuke her."

Here, Boaz engages in a universal rite of courtship that is still in use today: He shares an intimate meal with Ruth. It wasn't very elegant fare by the *haute cuisine* standards of our day—some roasted grain and bread dipped in vinegar—but then as now, the food itself is not the stuff of true romance. The meal is mere backdrop for conversation, for loving actions, for exchanging affectionate touches and glances. At the end of the meal, Ruth has enough food left to take some home to share with Naomi that night. His actions toward Ruth are extravagant, reminding us of the Lord's grace to us—there is always more than enough.

When Ruth rises to glean again, Boaz commands his workers to leave extra grain for her to gather. He gives instructions that Ruth should be allowed to go wherever she wants in the field, even near the grain that has been harvested. The workers are to make sure Ruth has plenty to glean—and more. Over and over, Boaz does what a true servant of God would do. She came seeking refuge under the wings of God, and he is God's servant, proactively meeting her needs. It is his delight to help Ruth. He is so thrilled with her gentle, sweet, gracious personality, and with the story he has heard of her heart and inner beauty, that he is honored to do anything he can to serve her.

As the story continues, Ruth arrives home with an entire ephah of grain—about three-fifths of a bushel. Naomi is astonished. "Where," she asks, "did you get all that grain?" Ruth relates the story of her meeting of Boaz, and a light goes on in Naomi's mind: "Boaz!" Naomi instantly recognizes the potential of this meeting: Boaz is a close kinsman, and thus (under the law of ancient Israel) he has a legal responsibility for these women.

One can imagine that Naomi probably proceeded to question Ruth: "Well, what about his wife? Oh, he told you she passed away when? So he's available, is he? And how do you feel about him? What did he say to you? Oh, that's a very good sign!" She sees that Boaz and Ruth are attracted to each other—and she begins to sense that something wonderful is happening. God is going beyond merely supplying the basics of existence. He is raining down blessings upon Ruth and Boaz—and some of those blessings are overflowing into Naomi's life as well!

By the end of chapter 2, crabby, embittered Naomi does something wonderful: She expresses thanks to God! In verses 19–20, we read:

> Then Ruth told her mother-in-law about the one at whose place she had been working. "The name of the man I worked with today is Boaz," she said.
>
> "The LORD bless him!" Naomi said to her daughter-in-law. "He has not stopped showing his kindness to the living and the dead."

Why does Naomi give thanks to the Lord? Because she sees that the circumstances have changed; now she can glimpse the possibilities of God's plan. She is still walking by sight rather than faith—but she is able to see with her eyes that God is working out His plan in the life of Ruth, Boaz, and Naomi. So this is a beautiful flowering of belief in Naomi's life.

But even more beautiful is the faith of Ruth, rooted not in what Ruth can see, but in her steadfast faith in an unseen God. Ruth believes in God's loving care even before she can see it in action, and that's why her example stands out. For Naomi, seeing is believing. For Ruth, believing is seeing.

God loves Naomi, of course, even though she can't believe in His provision and love until she can see it, touch it, and handle it. But how much better it is if we are able to begin with an attitude of faith and thankfulness to God, even before we have the tangible, visible proof of our faith. As Jesus said in John 20:29, "Because you have seen me, you have believed; blessed are those who have not seen and yet have believed."

Now, the scene that takes place between Ruth and Boaz isn't a very romantic scene in any classic sense. The idea of "love among the sheaves" may sound like a theme for a romance novel, but the reality is that the love story of Boaz and Ruth takes place under rather unromantic circumstances. Their touching mealtime conversation takes place within full view and earshot of a bunch of sweaty, soil-caked field hands. There is chaff all over the ground and dirt under everyone's fingernails. No matter. This is the beginning of a sweet and stirring heart-relationship that transcends all external circumstances.

In this story, we see the guiding hand of God, drawing a man and a woman together against all odds. At the same time, we see how God uses this new, emerging relationship between Boaz and Ruth to teach Naomi an important truth: God is real, God is active, God is involved in our lives, even amid seemingly hopeless circumstances. If we dedicate ourselves to becoming grateful, faithful, Christlike people, we give God the freedom to act and carry out his perfect, loving plan for our lives.

By the end of Ruth chapter 2, Naomi is just beginning to glimpse this truth in her own life. If you and I are attentive to what God has to teach us through the story of Ruth, then perhaps we are beginning to glimpse this truth for our own lives as well. We live by faith, not by sight. Seeing is not believing—believing is seeing!

CHAPTER 5

READY TO RECEIVE GOD'S GIFTS

Ruth 2

If you're a baby-boomer like me, you may remember the 1960s song "One Fine Day" by the Shirrelles, which was revived in a recent movie by the same title. It contains the lines:

> One fine day you'll look at me,
> and you will know our love was meant to be.

Is that where satisfying relationships begin? A look and a feeling that "our love was meant to be"? Is "true love" just something that strikes us out of the blue on "one fine day"? Judging from much of the romantic nonsense in today's media, you might think so!

In our culture, people tend to believe that good relationships come about magically, as a result of dumb luck, fate, or some arrangement of the stars. There are many romantic myths in our culture, all illogical, yet many of them passionately believed by millions of people. They believe that by consulting an astrologer, calling the Psychic Hot Line, or catching the bouquet or garter at a wedding, they can insure that they will find Mr. or Miss Right.

Others believe that technique is everything—that we find the great romance of our lives by learning how to manipulate, seduce, persuade, and captivate the opposite sex. It's simply a matter of the right line, or the right look, or the right attitude.

But the Bible teaches us that marriage is not a matter of fate or luck or technique. *It is a gift from God.* I have found that many people react against that statement. Perhaps they are in an unhappy marriage, so they ask, "How can you say that my marriage is a gift from God?" Or they are unmarried and lonely, so they ask, "Why has God passed me up? Why hasn't He given this gift to me?"

So I want to make this point at the outset: *Marriage is certainly not the only gift that comes from God.* What God wants us to learn about the gift of marriage from the story of Ruth and Boaz can be applied to *all* the gifts God gives us.

Think about it: If God wanted to make you the steward and manager of some important resource, how would He give you that gift? If He wanted to bring a new and wonderful friend into your life, how would He give you that gift? If He wanted to call you into a significant new ministry or vocation for Him, how would He give you that gift?

Answer: The same way He brought the gift of love, romance, and marriage into the life of Ruth and Boaz.

As we examine the mechanism God used to bring Ruth and Boaz together, as we see how each became God's gift to the other, we will learn something profound about the way God gives all of His gifts to us. So it is important that we understand that the story of Ruth is not just a story about love and marriage. It is a story about our love-relationship with God, and His grace and generosity toward us.

How God prepares us to receive His gifts

To really understand the gift that God gave to Boaz and Ruth, we need to go back in time to the very first time this gift was given—the first marriage between Adam and Eve. In the garden, God made a man with His hands, scooping up dust from the ground and molding it into a living, breathing being. The Hebrew verb used to describe the creation of Adam is the same verb used to describe the way a potter takes clay and molds it with his thumbs and fingers. The man Adam was the handiwork of God. The first man spent a period of time, perhaps even years, learning from God about the world He had created. God and the man walked and talked together. Even then, God was still in the process of forming the man with His words and His companionship.

The woman had much the same experience. God put the man to sleep, took a rib from his side, and fashioned the woman. She, too, was God's handiwork. And while the man was asleep, she enjoyed the intimacy of God's companionship by herself, just as Adam had. He talked to her, instructed her, and encouraged her. He fashioned her on the inside as well as the outside.

When the Lord had made them both as He wanted them to be, He brought them together and gave them in marriage to each other. The first marriage was not a matter of blind luck or manipulative technique. For those who love God and give Him free access to work in their lives, good marriages come as a gift from God. Why? Because when both the man and the woman allow Him to shape them according to His will, He is able to shape them and mold them into a perfect fit for each other. He fits each of them for the gift He is going to give them. His hands, His words, and His heart fashion them. Then, one fine day, He brings the two of them together into a setting where a relationship can begin that will last a lifetime.

We see this at the end of the marriage-making process between Adam and Eve in Genesis 2. There, we see that God wakes Adam up and gives Adam and Eve to each other—a very fine day indeed! And in Genesis 2:23, Adam says, "This is now bone of my bones and flesh of my flesh; she shall be called 'woman,' for she was taken out of man." In other words, "This is the one God has fashioned and shaped as the perfect fit for me. We have been made for each other by God."

That's what happens in Genesis, in the story of Adam and Eve. That's what happens in Ruth chapter 2. And it is also what can happen in your life and mine—if we will learn from this story and apply its truth to our lives. The challenge before us is to allow God to shape us and fit us and prepare us to receive the wonderful gift He has in store for us.

How Ruth made herself ready to receive God's gifts

Just as Ruth went into the field of Boaz to glean food, we can move through Ruth chapter 2, gleaning information about the kind of person Ruth was and the ways she prepared herself to receive God's unexpected gifts of grace. The narrative in chapter 2 gives us many key clues as to what Ruth was really like.

First, Ruth had to persuade Naomi that gleaning was a good idea. While Naomi didn't resist the idea, she failed to take any initiative in the matter. She was withdrawn, hurt, broken, and filled with self-pity, which she expressed at the end of chapter 1 with the gloomy pronouncement, "Don't call me Naomi. Call me Mara, call me Bitter. God has dealt bitterly with me." So Ruth approached her and said, "Naomi, there is one open door for people like us. We are poor, and the law of Israel says that the poor may go into the fields and glean. I'm going to trust that the one door God has opened is the door we ought to go through. I'm going to trust that He loves us, and that this is what He wants us to do."

Gleaning was a potentially dangerous thing to do, since this was the lawless, violent era of the judges. The poor took a risk going into the fields to glean, even though gleaning was their legal right. But Ruth believed that she lived in her the world of the God of Israel, that the Scriptures were trust-worthy, and that God would be faithful to His promises.

We are tempted, as we read this story, to think, "That was then, and this is now. God doesn't work that way any-more." But that's not true. The principles of the Bible are as true today as they were in the time of Ruth—that is why God has given us His Word. He wants us to learn from the lives of the people of the Old and New Testaments, and to apply the lessons of their lives to our own lives.

So how should we apply Ruth's godly perspective to our own setting, to our own problems and trials, so that we can become people of faith and gratitude, prepared and ready to receive God's gifts? Well, what are the problems you face right now? Perhaps it is an issue much like that of Ruth and Naomi, an issue of poverty or debt or wondering where your next paycheck will come from. Or maybe you face a blank wall of loneliness, of feeling ignored or rejected. Or maybe you feel your life is careening out of control, you are overwhelmed with responsibilities, pres-sures, and deadlines, and you feel you can't possibly keep up.

What would be the scriptural perspective that would prepare you to receive an urgently needed gift from God in the coming days? How could you make yourself ready, as Ruth did, to receive God's grace and generosity?

The first thing we notice about Ruth's attitude is that she placed no demands or expectations on God. She did not say, "Lord, Naomi and I have our backs to the wall, there's no money, no food, and no hope! Lord, you've got to come through by 9 a.m. tomorrow or our goose is cooked!" Ruth is willing to simply go out and glean and do what she has to do to get through one more day. She has no expectation that God will bring a wonderful man into her life. She places no demand or timetable on God. She is faithful to God and to Naomi—and she is patient.

A wise man once said, "God is never late—but He's never early either." Yes, God often seems to be late according to our schedule. But God wants us to learn to set our watches by His; instead, we tend to demand that He set His watch by ours! God won't always meet our deadlines—but in the cosmic scheme of things, our deadline is not the one that matters. It's His. And He always knows best, and He works out His plan for His own good and for the ultimate good of those who love Him. That paycheck, that relationship, that extra time or energy, or that deadline extension we need so badly is coming, it's on the way in God's good time, and it will be there when we need it. In the meantime, we can rely on God's grace to get along without it.

While we are waiting for God's gift for our lives, we should turn to Scripture for specific guidance in dealing with the particular circumstances we face. If, for example, we are feeling burned out, stressed out, and exhausted, we can turn to Hebrews 4:9–11, which tells us:

> There remains, then, a Sabbath-rest for the people of God; for anyone who enters God's rest also rests from his own work, just as God did from his. Let us, therefore, make every effort to enter that rest, so that no one will fall by following their example of disobedience.

God calls all of His people to His rest. Even amid the hassle and hubbub of our daily lives, we are called to live lives that are at rest on the inside, lives that are centered and at peace in Him. That is the open door God has provided for you and me as His people, living in a hurried, troubled world.

Maybe anxiety is your problem in life. Maybe you feel a sense of dread because of some worry, some circumstance, some person in your life, some inner struggle, or even some gnawing, nameless sense of uneasiness. If that is your problem, then turn to Philippians 4:6–7, which tells us:

> Do not be anxious about anything, but in everything, by
> prayer and petition, with thanksgiving, present your
> requests to God. And the peace of God, which transcends
> all understanding, will guard your hearts and your minds
> in Christ Jesus.

If you are anxious, and if you can find no other word of
peace from Scripture about your problem, then remember the
words of this passage: Pray, and receive God's transcendent
gift of peace.

Whatever our challenge, issue, or problem, we have all
the wisdom of Scripture available to us. That is the open
door through which we can walk, trusting and patiently
believing that this is our Father's world and that He keeps
His promises. We can wake up on a given day as Naomi did,
consumed with self-pity, unwilling to lift our eyes toward
God, unwilling to lift a hand to make our circumstances even
a little better—or we can say, "I have only one open door, but
that's enough. I'll walk through, and go where the Word of
God directs me to go. I'll live like a Christian instead of
being absorbed with myself."

That's the kind of woman Ruth was. We detect the handiwork of God in her life. She has been taught some hard lessons and has learned from suffering. Most of all, she has
been a pliant, moldable substance in the hands of the Great
Potter, and she has allowed God to shape her and prepare her
to be a vessel into which He can pour His wonderful, unexpected gift of grace. Had she resisted His lessons, had she
fought His efforts to shape and mold her character, she
would not have been the beautiful, gracious woman that so
captivated the eye of Boaz. She would not have been shaped
as a vessel into which God could pour His blessings.

I believe it truly was the beautiful spirit of Ruth that
Boaz found so entrancing. Remember, when they first met,
she was not alluringly attired, with her hair stunningly

arranged, her makeup meticulously applied, and just the right shade of lipstick. In her first encounter with Boaz, she had already been out working in the hot sun. She was tired and wringing with sweat. No doubt, she felt embarrassed and unattractive in this man's presence, seeing herself as bedraggled and dirty. She may have felt self-conscious about her strange accent, having come from the land of Moab.

But Boaz didn't judge her by any of those external criteria. He had heard about her. He had watched her. He had asked about her. And then he heard her speak, and witnessed first-hand the graciousness and sweetness of her character. He saw that this was a woman who had allowed God to shape her soul and to mold her into the perfect mate, the perfect fit, for his own life. Because she had allowed God to perform His work in her life, she was able to receive God's blessing—and she was able to be used by God to bless the life of Boaz.

How Boaz made himself ready to receive God's gifts

Now, let's look at Boaz and the way he made himself ready to receive God's blessing. I think it is important, first of all, that we take note of some of the details in the narrative. We see that Boaz is first shown giving his workers a blessing and a greeting, and we see that they bless and greet him in return. Why does the writer of this book record such a minor detail? To show something of the character of Boaz. From this greeting, we see that he was a man who lived his life as a blessing to others. He was interested in others and cared for others, and he was liked and respected in return.

Because he was attentive to people and interested in people, he noticed Ruth, a new person in his field among the workers and regular gleaners. If he had been a different kind of man, he might not have even noticed. But he was immediately attentive, because he was always attentive to people and interested in what God was doing in their lives. This is an important point because it indicates to us that when Boaz took notice of Ruth, it was not because he was sexually attracted to her. Rather, it was because he was always interested in *all* people, in their welfare, and in seeing God bless their lives. He viewed Ruth not as an object of sexuality, as many men immediately would, but as a *person*, as a living *soul*.

"Who is she?" he asked. A different sort of man might have complained, "Don't we have enough gleaners around here? Why doesn't she go to someone else's field? I could harvest more barley and make more money if it weren't for all these blankity-blank gleaners tramping through my field!" But that's not the attitude of Boaz. Instead, he inquires about Ruth because that is his way: He wants to know about the people in his sphere of influence, because he wants God to use him as a blessing in their lives. He thinks, *Here is another person God has brought into my life. If I knew something about her I might be able to help her receive God's best as well.* At this point, the attraction Boaz feels for Ruth is not sexual; it is spiritual.

When Boaz arose that morning, he had no idea that God was bringing a woman into his life, and that she would completely change his world and erase his loneliness. But Boaz had a lifestyle of expecting God to use him to do good—and it was that heart of a servant, that lifestyle of blessing others, that created the opportunity for God to work in his life. Do you see how the fingers of God have fashioned this man? He has been prepared over the years to be a good husband, and to share love with a good wife. He has been matured and sensitized, molded and fitted, to receive God's generous gift.

Then, after he learned who Ruth was, that she was the wonderful, loving young woman from Moab who loved God and served Naomi with steadfast loyalty, his interest intensified. Boaz knew that God rewarded people who lived like Ruth, people who lived to do good to others. Boaz said to himself, *If that's what God is doing, I want to be involved.*

Boaz prayed for Ruth to be blessed—and then he proceeded to make himself available to God as the agent of blessing in Ruth's life.

Walking through the door of blessing

There is a point in the story, somewhere between verses 11 and 12 of Ruth chapter 2, where the story takes a turn. Somewhere in those lines of dialogue between Ruth and Boaz, the spark of a holy and blessed romance ignites between them. In verse 12, Boaz speaks a very chaste and spiritual blessing to Ruth: "May the LORD repay you for what you have done. May you be richly rewarded by the LORD, the God of Israel, under whose wings you have come to take refuge."

Then, in verse 13, Ruth replies: "May I continue to find favor in your eyes, my lord. You have given me comfort and have spoken kindly to your servant—though I do not have the standing of one of your servant girls." She speaks gratefully, graciously, humbly, perhaps with eyes downcast—and Boaz feels his heart going out to her in a very special way. He is feeling something he hasn't felt in years—and so is she. It is the first stirring of romantic love.

In the next verse, we see Boaz doing more for Ruth than the usual blessing and help that he gives to all people. He shows her special attention at mealtime. He gives special instructions to his workers to show her deference and kindness. At this moment, kind and compassionate Boaz is showing Ruth a different quality of kindness and blessing than that which he normally accords all people. Ruth is special in his heart—and Boaz is special in her heart.

Boaz and Ruth are falling in love.

For these two people, who have allowed God to shape them and mold them and fit them for each other, that "one fine day" has arrived. God has brought them together. He has given them the amazing, unexpected gift of each other.

Reflecting on the story of Ruth and Boaz, I once asked my wife, Leslie, about our life together. "Do you remember a moment in our relationship," I asked, "like the moment Ruth and Boaz experience in Ruth 2:12 and 13?"

"I certainly do," she replied.

And just as she said that, I knew the moment she remembered.

Leslie and I had been friends long before we fell in love. We met while working at a Young Life camp, and became close friends during the next four years. It had been a good and important friendship, but it was one of a number of good friendships we each had within a common circle of Christian friends. We had never dated, and we had never really been together, just Leslie and I. We just didn't think about each other that way.

In the spring of 1970, I was planning to fly from California to Portland, Oregon, intending to go from there to Willamette University in Salem for a week of student ministry. At the same time, Leslie was at the end of her spring break and was returning to school in Seattle from her home in Walnut Creek, near San Francisco. We talked about our plans, and decided to take the same flight—I would keep her company as far as Portland, then she would fly on to Seattle after I got off the plane.

But God had other plans. He appointed a fog in Portland, so the plane was unable to make its scheduled stop in Oregon. As a result, I had to go on to Seattle with Leslie. There was no transportation back to Portland that day, so I was stranded in Seattle. I didn't mind—Leslie was a good friend, and she offered to show me around Seattle. At the end of the day, she let me spend the night on the floor of her place in Seattle.

When Leslie and I had stepped aboard that plane in California that morning, neither one of us had the least romantic notion about the other. But by the time I left Seattle and was heading to Portland, my original destination, I was definitely thinking in a very different way about my friendship with this young lady. And, I later found out, so was she.

Two years later, almost to the day, Leslie and I were married.

God delights to give good gifts to His children, including (but not limited to) the gift of marriage. Whatever your situation, whatever your need, God wants to give you gracious, generous gifts of His love. Are you preparing yourself right now to receive them? Are you listening to His Word and building it into your life and reordering your life according to His principles? Are you, for example, living your life by such life-molding, soul-transforming precepts as:

> "Be devoted to one another in brotherly love. Honor one another above yourselves" (Romans 12:10).

> "Do not let your hearts be troubled. Trust in God; trust also in me" (John 14:1).

> "Preach the Word; be prepared in season and out of season; correct, rebuke and encourage—with great patience and careful instruction" (2 Timothy 4:2).

> "Let us not give up meeting together, as some are in the habit of doing, but let us encourage one another—and all the more as you see the Day approaching" (Hebrews 10:25).

> "Be still, and know that I am God" (Psalm 46:10).

These are biblical admonitions to God's people. A person with a Ruth-like heart will arise in the morning and say, "I need to start the day, listening to His promises and admonitions, because I want His Word to shape my life, and I want my soul to be anchored to His promises. I know that

God is faithful to His promises—and I want to be faithful to God."

Ruth loved the Word of God, and Boaz trusted the working of the Spirit of God. He entered every situation with his eyes and ears open, watching and listening for opportunities to serve God and bless human lives. He noticed people and he sought their welfare. Is that the way you and I live our lives? If not—why not?

Good things—a new relationship, marriage, a new career or ministry, good friends, children, or the realization of a dream—don't just happen to us by blind luck or manipulation. All good things come as gifts from God. It is God who makes us ready to receive His gifts. It is God who prepares us and shapes us so that we can receive His gifts with gratitude and to use them with grace.

Someday, in heaven, we will look back on our lives, and many things that seem murky today will then be crystal clear. Will we see all the times God wanted us to receive His gifts, but we were too stubborn, too self-willed to receive them? Will we see all the times God opened the door of blessing for us, but we walked past or slammed the door shut? Perhaps we have passed by the field of Boaz again and again, not realizing that the gift was within our grasp all along. Perhaps we have been so consumed with self-promotion or self-pity or self-will that we couldn't even see the gift God wanted to give us.

Let's pray that God will open our eyes, illumine our understanding, and show us His door of blessing. And let us be willing to do God's will and allow Him to shape us into the kind of men and women He wants us to be, the vessels He wants to pour His blessings into.

Ruth listened to God and entered the open door God made for her. So did Boaz. Now the question that confronts us is: Will we?

Does the Word of God compel us and motivate us to get out of our self-absorption, move beyond our comfort zone, pay attention to others, and become a blessing in the lives of the people around us? Do we believe the Spirit of God is at work in our generation, and that God wants to use us as a blessing to the people around us? These are the ways we allow God's hand to shape us and mold us and make us the kind of people He wants us to be.

God is a giver of good gifts. He has reserved His best for us, blessings beyond our ability to imagine! But he can only give His gifts to us if we are ready and prepared to receive them.

CHAPTER 6

MANAGING AND
MEASURING GOD

Ruth 2

Time for a quick spiritual quiz. Simply answer the following questions by checking the appropriate box, yes or no:

Yes/NoQuestion:

❑❑ Have you ever set out to serve the Lord, only to realize later that your real motive was to be noticed by other people?

❑❑ Have you ever claimed to be acting in Christlike love for another person, only to realize later that your real motive was to control or manipulate the feelings or actions of the person you claimed to love?

❑❑ Have you ever, as a parent, gone out of your way to do something or provide something for your children, believing you were doing so purely out of love, when in reality you were subtly competing and keeping up with other parents?

❏❏ Have you ever shared a prayer request or offered to pray for someone, when your real motive was a subtle desire to gossip about that person?

Our motives are so slippery and deceptive. Being blind to our own motives is a trap we all fall into from time to time—myself included! Our true motivations can be so subtle and so well hidden from our conscious awareness that it is almost impossible for us to see them for what they are.

How do we learn to see through the blind spots in our lives? Sometimes what is hidden from our own awareness can only be seen by someone outside of ourselves. That is why we need other Christians around us, involved in our lives, watching our behavior, holding us accountable for our actions before God. That is why we sometimes need to go to a pastor, counselor, or Christian therapist for counseling and insight into the hidden motives and issues that hurt us and baffle us.

But God also holds up a mirror to our lives through the stories he has given us in His Word. Sometimes when we see a particular problem in a person in the Bible, God can use that story to help us discover that same sin or blind spot in ourselves.

The New Testament book of Hebrews tells us, "But encourage one another daily, as long as it is called Today, so that none of you may be hardened by sin's deceitfulness" (Hebrews 3:13). Our sinful nature is so deceptive that it easily dupes us into turning our best intentions into acts of evil, destructiveness, and sin. It can twist our prayers into gossip, our acts of kindness into self-congratulation and pride, our service to God into a pseudo-religious show.

How do we discover and eliminate the blind spots in our lives? That is yet another theme that emerges from this rich and enchanting story we find in the second chapter of Ruth.

Blindness and lack of faith

Most of Ruth 2 is taken up with the story of the beautiful meeting between Boaz and Ruth. But near the end of the chapter, a conversation between Ruth and Naomi brings Naomi center-stage once again. We will see, as we take a close look at this section of Ruth chapter 2, that while Naomi may not be the most likable and enjoyable character in the book of Ruth, she is probably the one with whom we most easily identify. From my own experience, I can say that I understand Naomi the best of all the characters in this book, because she is the character most like me.

It is this very identification with Naomi that God uses to reflect our lives back to us, saying, "Does this look familiar? Do you see Naomi's blind spot and sin? Don't her problems and failings look a lot like your own? Yes, it's easy to see Naomi's blindness and lack of faith—but doesn't that ring a bell in your own heart?"

Notice, first of all, that Naomi is clearly not an evil or mean-spirited person. She declares blessings, makes pronouncements, and gives advice. Like you and me, she wants to do what is right. In verses 17–23 we read:

> So Ruth gleaned in the field until evening. Then she threshed the barley she had gathered, and it amounted to about an ephah. She carried it back to town, and her mother-in-law saw how much she had gathered. Ruth also brought out and gave her what she had left over after she had eaten enough.
>
> Her mother-in-law asked her, "Where did you glean today? Where did you work? Blessed be the man who took notice of you!"
>
> Then Ruth told her mother-in-law about the one at whose place she had been working. "The name of the man I worked with today is Boaz," she said.
>
> "The LORD bless him!" Naomi said to her daughter-in-law. "He has not stopped showing his kindness to the

living and the dead." She added, "That man is our close relative; he is one of our kinsman-redeemers."

Then Ruth the Moabitess said, "He even said to me, 'Stay with my workers until they finish harvesting all my grain.' "

Naomi said to Ruth her daughter-in-law, "It will be good for you, my daughter, to go with his girls, because in someone else's field you might be harmed."

So Ruth stayed close to the servant girls of Boaz to glean until the barley and wheat harvests were finished. And she lived with her mother-in-law.

We have a number of Naomi's speeches recorded throughout the book of Ruth, and again and again we see the words of a woman who means well, but whose thinking and words continually miss the mark. She frequently makes judgments about God and His involvement in Naomi's life that are pessimistic and untrue. She gives well-intentioned but bad advice.

What the second chapter of Ruth clearly presents to us is a vivid contrast between two believers, Naomi and Ruth—a contrast in the quality of their faith and the faithfulness with which they live their lives. The book of Ruth shows us how two trouble-stricken widows respond in very different ways to essentially the same dire circumstances in life. Ruth lives by faith, and because of her faith, she is willing to takes bold risks for the sake of her God, trusting in the unseen realities of His promises. Naomi, however, lives by sight, and responds out of a lack of risky faith, and out of pessimism.

The contrast between Ruth and Naomi is the key to understanding and interpreting this book.

Measuring and managing

I feel a great kinship to Naomi. Her speeches are speeches I could make. Like most people, I can take a certain amount of suffering for a certain period of time. I seek to follow the counsel of the New Testament passage that tells us:

> Consider it pure joy, my brothers, whenever you face trials of many kinds, because you know that the testing of your faith develops perseverance (James 1:2–3).

When trials come my way, I ask God to help me maintain a joyful attitude, knowing that this trial is going to make me a stronger Christian. But look at the trial Naomi goes through—famine, dislocation from home, widowhood, the death of her children, poverty, uncertainty about the future—and this trial goes on and on for ten years! Certainly, there must be limits to what God expects us to endure! Certainly, a ten-year trial is too long! If I had been in Naomi's shoes, I'm not sure my response would have been any more godly than hers.

Shouldn't God be called to account for giving Naomi such a hard assignment? Naomi certainly thinks so! That is why we hear Naomi, in Ruth 1:13 and 20–21, putting God on trial and measuring his performance:

> "It is more bitter for me than for you, because the LORD's hand has gone out against me!"

> "Don't call me Naomi," she told them. "Call me Mara, because the Almighty has made my life very bitter." I went away full, but the LORD has brought me back empty. Why call me Naomi? The LORD has afflicted me; the Almighty has brought misfortune upon me."

Naomi has judged God, and has found His performance inadequate. "God hasn't carried out His promises," she says, in effect. "He isn't who He claims to be, He has hurt me and leveled me with misfortunes." Naomi has measured God, and the conclusion she draws is one of bitterness.

Naomi not only measures God, she also tries to manage God. She wants God to give her the reins of control. She wants Him to provide the wherewithal for her to make her way in life—then leave it up to her to take care of business. I read the words of Naomi as she tries to manage God, and something resonates within me. And suddenly I realize why the words of Naomi sound so familiar: I do the very same thing!

In my own life, I have also tried to measure God and manage God. This story is written so that people like Naomi—and people like me—can recognize ourselves and see that there is another way to live. God wants us to trust Him with our lives. He wants us to truly live by faith—not by a cold religious code.

The advice of Naomi

Let's quickly review some of the well-intentioned but faithless advice Naomi has given in Ruth 1.

After Naomi and her two daughters-in-law, Ruth and Orpah, were widowed, Naomi offered them a virtuoso feat of rational assessment, laced with pungent sarcasm. She examined her own life and in words to this effect, she snapped, "My husband is dead—and even if I could instantly marry and have children (like that could ever happen!), would the two of you be able to wait until those children grow up and become men for you to marry?!"

She then lists a number of reasons why these young women should not look to her for help, saying in effect, "I have no cards left to play, I have no more influence. I am poor and without hope. I can't do anything for you. There is no shred of hope left for you here with me. Go back to your homeland, and at least you'll have a chance for a future." That advice culminates in Ruth 1:15, where Naomi tells Ruth, "Look, your sister-in-law is going back to her people and her gods. Go back with her."

Well-intentioned advice? Absolutely! But wise and godly advice? Absolutely not! In fact, Naomi couldn't have possibly offered Ruth worse advice than that. Had Ruth listened to Naomi, she never would have gone to Bethlehem, she never would have gleaned in the fields, and she never would have met Boaz. And with 3,000 years of perspective, we can see that there is even more at stake in Ruth's decision than her own future.

If this were a play, the people in the audience would be yelling at Ruth, "Don't listen to Naomi! Don't do it, Ruth! If you follow her advice, there will be no King David, and there will be no Messiah!" Because, as Matthew 1:5 tells us, the marriage of Boaz and Ruth produces a line of descendants which includes King David and Jesus the Messiah. So, from a limited human perspective, Naomi seems to be giving good, logical, hard-headed advice—but from a divine perspective, her advice couldn't have been more wrongheaded.

Next we hear Naomi's conclusions about herself. Twice Naomi makes pronouncements about her life and circumstances. Look at 1:13: "It is more bitter for me than for you, because the Lord's hand has gone out against me!" That statement is wrong on two counts:

First, it is not harder for Naomi than Ruth and Orpah. Ruth and Orpah have been given the same set of hard circumstances as Naomi. They, too, are poor, widowed, and childless. Ruth is a foreigner without any standing or prospects for the future. It is Naomi's self-pity and self-absorption that makes her say this—but the details of the story tell us it just isn't so.

Second, the hand of the Lord has not been set against Naomi. Yes, it would certainly be very difficult to trust God after a long, punishing trial like the one Naomi had gone through. But what Naomi didn't know was that God was doing the best possible thing. Naomi didn't realize that God was arranging events so that she would become one of the great matriarchs of faith in the history of Israel. God was doing good to her.

And consider that statement Naomi makes in Ruth 1:21— "I went away full, but the LORD has brought me back empty. Why call me Naomi [pleasant]? The LORD has afflicted me; the Almighty has brought misfortune upon me." Here again, Naomi was drawing a reasonable conclusion. I would have probably drawn a similar conclusion in her place. Her views were based on years of painful observation of life—yet her views were *wrong*. God had not turned against Naomi—and she had not returned empty. She came back to Bethlehem with a daughter-in-law, and that is the key to everything in this story. She didn't have sons and she didn't have a husband, but she had the one through whom God was going to provide. She just couldn't see God's provision in her life.

Every time Naomi states an opinion or offers advice, her analysis is called into question by the story itself. But there is someone beside her—her daughter-in-law, Ruth—whose views and actions contrast with Naomi's at every stage. Though Ruth respects her mother-in-law, it is clear that Ruth does not accept Naomi's faithless advice. Instead, she lovingly says, "No, Naomi. I'm not going to leave you. I will stay with you and trust your God, even though you are not able to trust Him."

And Ruth's words imply an even deeper truth: "I'm not going to give in to bitterness," she seems to indicate. "The hand of the LORD hasn't been set against us. We can't see Him, but we can trust Him. We can't see yet what He is going to do, but we can trust that He will do it." We see commitment, love, faithfulness, and awareness of God in the life and attitude of the younger woman.

Naomi's response versus Ruth's

In Ruth 2:17–23, Ruth brings back to Naomi the ephah of barley she has gleaned—and the story of the landowner who showed her kindness, Boaz. Now that she can hold the proof of God's goodness in a bushel basket, Naomi is able to give praise to God, while blessing Boaz: "The LORD bless him! God still shows His kindness to the living and the dead." Then Naomi tells Ruth, "The man, Boaz, is one of our closest relatives." And she adds that, for her own safety, Ruth should stay close to the servant girls of Boaz when she gleans.

It's important to note that all of the events of Ruth 2 take place on a single day. It is also important to recognize that this chapter provides us with a strong contrast between two different attitudes, the attitude of Ruth versus the attitude of Naomi. Ruth is one kind of person, Naomi is another.

This is not to ridicule Naomi for struggling with her faith. In fact, one of the points that comes across in this chapter is that God desires to *help* people who struggle to have faith. He is committed to them and loves them. He knows that human beings will try to measure Him and manage Him—but He is committed to enabling us to grow beyond this immature stage in our faith.

What shall we make of Naomi's reaction?

We learn, first of all, that a lack of trust and a lack of faith in God can cause us to miss out. By staying home and nursing her bitterness, Naomi missed out on the events in the field of Boaz. Now, if Ruth had not come back from Moab, Naomi would have had to go glean for herself in order to survive. The only reason Naomi didn't glean is because faithful Ruth was willing to do it for her. But God had a plan of redemption in the lives of Ruth and Naomi, and the only way for them to experience it was for Ruth to go out in faith to glean in the field—then return to Naomi and tell her what God had done in the field.

And that is what takes place. Ruth returns with a huge bag of barley and the roasted grain, and Naomi asks her to relate the events of the day. Clearly, Naomi is especially fascinated by the astonishing amount of food Ruth has brought home. She wants to know who is responsible for it. And then she issues a blessing on the one, as yet unnamed, who provided all this bounty.

In Ruth 2:8–9, we see that Ruth's response to God's provision was different from Naomi's:

> So Boaz said to Ruth, "My daughter, listen to me. Don't go and glean in another field and don't go away from here. Stay here with my servant girls. Watch the field where the men are harvesting, and follow along after the girls. I have told the men not to touch you. And whenever you are thirsty, go and get a drink from the water jars the men have filled."
>
> At this, she bowed down with her face to the ground. She exclaimed, "Why have I found such favor in your eyes that you notice me—a foreigner?"

Notice that, at this point, all Boaz has done is give her the rights she already enjoyed as a gleaner—nothing more, nothing above and beyond the call of duty. He has provided water for her, and he has insisted that she be treated with respect. But he has not as yet given her any gifts—no ephah of barley, no meal, and no hint that more blessings would follow.

Yet Ruth responds with overflowing gratitude. She falls on her face before him in gratitude for the mere crumbs of kindness Boaz has shown. It is interesting that her first question is not, "Who are you?" but "Who am I, a foreigner, that you should take notice of me?" This question is so typical of Ruth—a question that expresses both her gratitude and her utter humility. She is grateful to both God and to the man of God who has helped her—and nowhere in this question do we sense any expectation of further benefit.

Later, in Ruth 3:16–17, we will witness a scene in which Ruth returns again meeting with Boaz at the threshing floor:

When Ruth came to her mother-in-law, Naomi asked, "How did it go, my daughter?"

Then she told her everything Boaz had done for her and added, "He gave me these six measures of barley, saying, 'Don't go back to your mother-in-law empty-handed.' "

Both Boaz and Ruth were aware that Naomi had difficulty trusting in God's provision and care unless it came in a tangible form that could be measured. So Boaz wisely told Ruth, "Be sure and go back with something tangible so Naomi's heart can be encouraged." We see this same issue in Naomi's life at the end of Ruth chapter 2, where Naomi declares a blessing on Boaz—a blessing on Ruth's and Naomi's benefactor, in response to his generosity. Here again, there is a clear contrast between the spirit of Ruth and the spirit of Naomi. Ruth expresses gratitude even before she has received a tangible benefit; Naomi only expresses gratitude when the tangible benefit is in her hands.

Naomi takes matters into her own hands

Naomi is pleased to learn the name of the man who helped Ruth—and she immediately grasps the implications. Someone in the extended family will need to take responsibility for the widows and buy back Elimelech's property. That is why Naomi says, "The LORD bless Boaz! God has not stopped showing his kindness to the living and the dead. That man is our close relative; he is one of our kinsman-redeemers."

"The living" are Naomi and Ruth. "The dead" are Naomi's late husband, Elimelech, and her two sons. By doing good to the widows, the kinsman-redeemer will fulfill the dead men's responsibility to take care of the family property and the poor widowed women.

Here again, we see a contrast of attitudes—a contrast between what Naomi says in this passage versus what Ruth and Boaz said in the field. When Ruth says, "Why do you care for me?" Boaz does not say, "Because I'm a relative." He could have said, "Because I'm of the family of Elimelech, and we're responsible for you." Instead, he said something much more profound:

> "I've been told all about what you have done for your mother-in-law since the death of your husband— how you left your father and mother and your homeland and came to live with a people you did not know before. May the LORD repay you for what you have done. May you be richly rewarded by the LORD, the God of Israel, under whose wings you have come to take refuge."

In other words, Boaz says, "It's because you love your mother-in-law," and Boaz may have known that Naomi was not a very lovable lady. "And," he goes on, "it's because you have adopted the people of Israel, and you love the God of Israel, having sought refuge in Him. I'm not doing this because of a legal obligation to the family, but because I love God, and I love those who love Him."

In contrast, although Naomi wishes Boaz well and gives God credit for this good fortune, she is still in a scheming mode, hoping to have an influence on the outcome of events. "Since Boaz is a family member," she reasons, "I now have means to pull some strings and make things happen." Whereas in chapter 1, Naomi felt helpless, powerless, and without influence, she now believes she has some cards to play—and she intends to play them.

We see the culmination of Naomi's manipulative approach to life in Ruth 3:1:

> One day Naomi her mother-in-law said to her, "My daughter, should I not try to find a home for you, where you will be well provided for?"

Naomi is saying, in effect, "I'm taking matters into my own hands. God's managed things up to this point, but now it's time for me to step in and play matchmaker. Since God can't be trusted to get the job done, I'm going to make sure you have security and a home." Once again, if this were a play, everyone in the audience would be hollering, "No, Ruth! Don't do it! Don't listen to her!"

And sure enough, as Ruth chapter 3 unfolds, we will find once again that Naomi's advice is unwise. Every time Naomi takes matters into her own hands, draws her own conclusions, or gives directions to others, an alarm should go off in our minds. We should wonder, "What is God's plan for this situation?" Naomi continually tries to wrest control of the situation from God.

When Naomi offers to scheme a way for Ruth to find a home and security, we should immediately sense that something is wrong with Naomi's thinking. After all, where in this entire story have we seen Naomi provide security for anyone? In chapter 1, she gave up on God and any hope that God might provide through the people in Bethlehem. She tried to send both of her daughters-in-law back to Moab—and one of them, Orpah, went.

Naomi hasn't provided for Ruth—she has been the recipient of Ruth's commitment and love! It was Ruth who went out to glean for her, and who has been providing security for her. It was Boaz who generously provided food for her. And ultimately, it was God who generously provided everything—including the opportunity for love to blossom between Ruth and Boaz. Up until now, Naomi has provided exactly zilch. Instead of providing, she has been on the receiving end. Worse, she has even resisted being positively involved in the lives of other people.

And now she's going to take over God's job and start providing a home and security for Ruth? I don't think so! Clearly, we need to be very suspicious of any plan or advice that Naomi offers. Naomi is convinced that she is doing good things for good reasons, and that her good intentions will produce good results. But she keeps leaving God out of the equation.

God breaks through

At this point, do you begin to see your own image reflected in the personality of Naomi? I certainly do!

Don't we often measure God's performance against our own standards, our own schedule, our own agenda? And when He doesn't meet our performance criteria, do we say, "Lord, You know more than I do—I humbly submit to your wise, loving, perfect will"? Or do we more often say, "God, You don't know what it's like to go through these circumstances! You're not taking care of this situation! You really blew it! Let me take over!"

So we measure God and we manage God. We don't trust that God is truly in control, so we seize control. That is the way of Naomi—and all too often, it is our way, too.

But that is not the way of Ruth. She gives God control over her circumstances because she trusts that He is all-loving, all-knowing, and all-powerful. She willingly slides from the driver's seat to the passenger seat of her life, and allows God to take the wheel.

The Naomis of the world—people like you and me—have a lot to learn about trust. Many of us have hearts that are hardened by the deceitfulness of sin and self-will—and we need to have our sin-hardened, self-hardened hearts softened. And that is what the book of Ruth is about: God's ability to break through the hardness of our self-willed hearts, His ability to illuminate our blind spots, His ability to break us of our need to control, His ability to shore up our weakened faith and enlarge our diminished capacity for trust.

Naomi is not alone in her struggle to trust God and give Him control of her life. There are others in Scripture who struggle in similar ways. Job's story and Naomi's story are very similar. Both Job and Naomi have been dealt crushing, catastrophic blows in life. Their trials come straight out of the blue, and seemingly for no good reason. Finally, Job, like Naomi, shakes his fist at God and says:

> He throws me into the mud,
> > and I am reduced to dust and ashes.
> "I cry out to you, O God, but you do not answer;
> > I stand up, but you merely look at me.
> You turn on me ruthlessly;
> > with the might of your hand you attack me.
> You snatch me up and drive me before the wind;
> > you toss me about in the storm.
> I know you will bring me down to death,
> > to the place appointed for all the living."
> > > > > (Job 30:19–23)

At the end of the book, we see that Job, having railed against God, is caught up in a whirlwind and God takes him on a guided tour of the creation. God shows him the foundation of the seas, the stars in the sky, the ostrich, the crocodile, and the hippopotamus. Then God asks him, "Job, who are you in light of all this?" And Job, the Naomi-like man who wanted to measure and manage God, replies:

> "My ears had heard of you
> > but now my eyes have seen you.
> Therefore I despise myself
> > and repent in dust and ashes."
> > > > > (Job 42:5–6)

In other words, Job says that once he had merely heard of God, he merely had academic knowledge of God—but having gone through suffering, Job has become personally acquainted with God, he has seen God eye to eye. Through terrible circumstances, Job learned that God was worthy of praise and trust, and he repented in all humility of his former questioning and mistrust of God.

The disciples of Jesus had a similar experience while they were sailing upon the Sea of Galilee. In Mark 4:37–41, we read:

> A furious squall came up, and the waves broke over the boat, so that it was nearly swamped. Jesus was in the stern, sleeping on a cushion. The disciples woke him and said to him, "Teacher, don't you care if we drown?"
>
> He got up, rebuked the wind and said to the waves, "Quiet! Be still!" Then the wind died down and it was completely calm.
>
> He said to his disciples, "Why are you so afraid? Do you still have no faith?"
>
> They were terrified and asked each other, "Who is this? Even the wind and the waves obey him!"

Through the trials and storms of life, our Lord allows us to see more of Himself than we could in times of peace and ease. He rebukes our timidity by confronting us with the inadequacy of our faith in contrast with the complete adequacy of His love and power. He confounds our meager attempts to measure and manage Him. He is beyond all measurement, beyond all human management. He is Almighty God.

Remember the story of how Martha accused the Lord of failure. In Luke 10:40–42, we read:

> But Martha was distracted by all the preparations that had to be made. She came to him and asked, "Lord, don't you care that my sister has left me to do the work by myself? Tell her to help me!"
>
> "Martha, Martha," the Lord answered, "you are worried and upset about many things, but only one thing is needed. Mary has chosen what is better, and it will not be taken away from her."

Jesus is telling her, "Martha, are you saying I don't care? How could you say that? You need to know that there is something better than what you have chosen." In that moment, Jesus breaks through Martha's world-view, showing her that what she wants is not what she truly needs. He has not come to meet her wants but to meet her real needs. And what Martha needs is to know Him, to trust Him, to sit at His feet and learn from Him.

And that brings us back to Naomi. She attempts to control God and circumstances. She blames Him for her troubles. She plans and manipulates—even after God has already begun to show His loving provision for Naomi and Ruth. By the end of this tale, Naomi will hold her baby grandson in her arms. When she holds that baby, she will finally have a breakthrough of faith.

For those of us who are like Naomi, who charge off on our own path, claiming to know God's will, trying to prod Him into doing what we want while moving in the wrong direction, coming to flawed conclusions, and giving bad advice—the book of Ruth offers hope. Our faith may be tiny and frail—but God wants to do a great work in our lives. He may have to take us through the storm or through a time of famine—but in the end, it will all have been for our good, for the strengthening of our faith. One day, we will be able to conclude with Job that before we had only heard of God, but now we have seen Him with our own eyes. Before, God was a doctrinal statement; but now He is a living, caring Father.

The moment we learn to stop measuring and managing God, the moment we begin to simply trust Him, that's the moment we stop living like Naomi, and start living like Ruth. And when we live like Ruth—truly trusting God and giving Him the steering wheel of our lives—then He is able to direct our lives and to take us to a place of true blessing and joy.

CHAPTER 7

THE LANGUAGE OF LOVE

Ruth 2 and 3

I once received a phone call from a good friend, a Jewish Christian who had once been a member of Peninsula Bible Church. He had emigrated to Israel and joined the Israeli Army. When the phone rang at my home in California, it was morning—but my Israeli friend was calling in the middle of the night on a cellular phone from his patrol post on the border of Lebanon. After we finished talking, I marveled at this age of communication we live in!

We live at a time in which words fly around the globe at the speed of light. Our lives are inundated with speech and data. At the flip of a switch or the touch of a computer key, we can receive e-mail or hear news and commentary from the farthest, most obscure reaches of our planet—even the land that Abraham, Jacob, and Jesus once walked.

Yet, despite the torrent of words all around us, it is amazing to realize how little connection there often is between people. How many words we hear—but how few of those words penetrate to the heart. The language of love, the language of the heart, remains as elusive for most people today as it was three thousand years ago. It's a problem that technology cannot solve.

Fortunately, the problem has already been solved for us in the book of Ruth. As we examine the conversations between Ruth and Boaz, we will find solutions to our own communication problems that will serve us just as well today, in this age of cellular phones and the Internet, as it served these two lovers in ancient Israel. We will re-read and re-examine two conversations between Ruth and Boaz, one that is found in Ruth chapter 2, and one in chapter 3. We will see that the book of Ruth, which is so multi-dimensional, so applicable to our lives in so many ways, is also a powerfully practical book on the art of communication, connection, and conversation.

From the heart, to the heart

Most of the book of Ruth is talk. We hear Ruth talking to Naomi, Naomi talking to the women of the town, Ruth and Boaz talking to each other, and Boaz talking to the men of the town. In fact, as you read through the book of Ruth, you will discover that more than half of the verses in the book are in the form of dialogue, one person directly addressing another. This is a book of conversation, and it is important for us to hear what each character in the book is saying, and what their words reveal about their attitudes and their feelings.

In this chapter, we are going back over passages we have already examined in Ruth 2 and 3 and considering them from a different angle. I think a key passage to begin with is Ruth 2:13, which contains a phrase that is obscured in most English translations. In the New International Version, used throughout this study, Ruth says to Boaz on the first day they meet, "You have given me comfort and have spoken kindly to your servant." In the King James Version of that verse, Ruth says, "Thou hast spoken friendly unto thine hand-maid." But a literal rendering of what is written in the original Hebrew language of this verse is very instructive: "You have spoken to the heart of your handmaiden."

One reason these words are difficult to translate is that heart language is always difficult to say and difficult to hear. The heart that has been spoken to is vulnerable—and it is difficult to be emotionally vulnerable when others are around to hear. Yet Ruth and Boaz—who are strangers meeting in an open field, surrounded by other people who are listening in—do not hesitate to be vulnerable with each other. They speak candidly and directly. They speak the language of the heart.

Communication that connects with another person, and which speaks from the heart and to the heart, is not just a matter of having social skills, or glib words, and the ability to orate with eloquence. It is simply the ability to be honest and real.

Jesus made an important observation, recorded in Matthew 12:34–35: "For out of the overflow of the heart the mouth speaks. The good man brings good things out of the good stored up in him, and the evil man brings evil things out of the evil stored up in him." The mouth speaks what is in the heart. No matter how skilled an evil person is at sounding good, hearers will eventually find out what is in the heart. What is inside a person inevitably reveals itself through that person's words. The same is true of the good person. The good that is stored within a good person will be evident for all to see.

Words that lead to intimacy

Unfortunately, most of the examples and role models in our popular culture of man-woman relations are of relationships that are distorted and dysfunctional. Our world is aching for examples of people bringing good words out of a storehouse of godliness. As we consider these two conversations between Ruth and Boaz, we will witness the revelation of their hearts and their character. These are two good, godly people. They have learned the lessons of trusting God and loving others. By choosing to live lives of obedience and trust in God, they have developed character traits of courage, righteousness, and grace. They know how to bring forth the goodness that is within them. The first conversation between Ruth and Boaz is found in Ruth 2:8–16:

> So Boaz said to Ruth, "My daughter, listen to me. Don't go and glean in another field and don't go away from here. Stay here with my servant girls. Watch the field where the men are harvesting, and follow along after the girls. I have told the men not to touch you. And whenever you are thirsty, go and get a drink from the water jars the men have filled."
>
> At this, she bowed down with her face to the ground. She exclaimed, "Why have I found such favor in your eyes that you notice me—a foreigner?"
>
> Boaz replied, "I've been told all about what you have done for your mother-in-law since the death of your husband—how you left your father and mother and your homeland and came to live with a people you did not know before. May the LORD repay you for what you have done. May you be richly rewarded by the LORD, the God of Israel, under whose wings you have come to take refuge."
>
> "May I continue to find favor in your eyes, my lord," she said. "You have given me comfort and have spoken kindly to your servant—though I do not have the standing of one of your servant girls."
>
> At mealtime Boaz said to her, "Come over here. Have some bread and dip it in the wine vinegar."
>
> When she sat down with the harvesters, he offered her some roasted grain. She ate all she wanted and had some left over. As she got up to glean, Boaz gave orders to his men, "Even if she gathers among the sheaves, don't embarrass her. Rather, pull out some stalks for her from the bundles and leave them for her to pick up, and don't rebuke her."

The second conversation is found in Ruth 3:8–13. It takes place the night of the harvest party, when Ruth has gone to the threshing floor and is lying at Boaz's feet:

> In the middle of the night something startled the man, and he turned and discovered a woman lying at his feet.
> "Who are you?" he asked.
> "I am your servant Ruth," she said. "Spread the corner of your garment over me, since you are a kinsman-redeemer."
> "The LORD bless you, my daughter," he replied. "This kindness is greater than that which you showed earlier: You have not run after the younger men, whether rich or poor. And now, my daughter, don't be afraid. I will do for you all you ask. All my fellow townsmen know that you are a woman of noble character. Although it is true that I am near of kin, there is a kinsman-redeemer nearer than I. Stay here for the night, and in the morning if he wants to redeem, good; let him redeem. But if he is not willing, as surely as the LORD lives I will do it. Lie here until morning."

This is the heart language of those who are falling in love. These are conversations that lead to genuine human intimacy.

Notice, first, that there is no hint of awkwardness when Ruth and Boaz talk to each other. There have been times and places in human history in which men and women occupied almost entirely separate arenas. They knew so little about each other and had so little to do with each other that their conversations were stilted, awkward, or nonexistent. Even today, we hear that men and women come from different planets and communicate across a gulf that is light-years across—"Men are from Mars, women are from Venus."

A popular pastime in our culture is to "bash" the opposite gender. Being a man, it would be unseemly and unChristian for me to indulge in "woman-bashing," but here are a few "male-bashing" remarks, making the rounds on the Internet, that may bring a smile to your lips (particularly if you are a woman!):

Q: What is the thinnest book in the world?
A: *What Men Know About Women.*

Q: What's the difference between men and government bonds?
A: Bonds mature.

Q: How many men does it take to change a roll of toilet paper?
A: Who knows? It's never happened before.

Q: What do you call 144 men in one room?
A. Gross stupidity.

Q: What do you call a man with half a brain?
A: Gifted.

Q: What did God say after creating man?
A: "I'll get it right next time."

Did you hear about the man who won the gold medal at the Olympics? He was so proud, he had it bronzed.

As a man, I have to say there's not a word of truth in any of those remarks! (Well, maybe just a little.) This collection of "male-bashing" jokes illustrates in a light-hearted way the very real division between men and women in contemporary society. There is a guardedness and defensiveness between men and women today. Even though both genders increasingly occupy the same place (particularly the workplace) and do many of the same activities, they interact warily, anxiously avoiding any misstep or misunderstanding. Conversations between men and women are reduced to a functional and utilitarian interaction that deals only in basic facts and avoids real feelings.

But Boaz and Ruth don't have any problem with guardedness, awkwardness, or misunderstanding in their speech. They don't seem to regard the opposite gender as an alien species. They just talk to each other, speaking what is in their hearts. To me, that is encouraging. God wants men and women to talk to each other, to treat each other with respect and appreciation.

It is important to observe that both Ruth and Boaz express gratitude for an unexpected gift. They are both grateful for a blessing they have received, because they didn't anticipate the blessing. In Ruth 2:10, the first thing Ruth does when Boaz shows kindness to her is fall on her face and say, "I'm a foreigner, a nobody. Why would you be so good to me?" Ruth was not angling for Boaz's favor, and Boaz had no ulterior motive in reaching out to her.

Boaz has the same experience of gratitude when Ruth finally raises the question of marriage. In Ruth 3:10, he says to Ruth, in effect, "Your last kindness is better than the one before. I expected you to be interested in young men. I didn't think you would want someone like me." And it is his surprise and gratitude that we hear when they whisper to each other on the threshing floor. Gratitude—pure, unfeigned, and straight from the heart—is one of the most beautiful of all expressions of the human heart.

Relating as equals

Another important observation we can make from these two conversations between Ruth and Boaz is that they relate to each other as equals. There is a deep mutual respect and admiration, despite the many factors that distinguish them from each other—that might even separate them from each other. One is a man, the other is a woman. One is older, the other is younger. One is a Jew, the other is a Moabite. One is wealthy, the other is poor to the point of destitution. Despite all these factors that would seem to separate them from each other, they treat each other as equals.

Ruth refuses the false, manipulative form of "submission" that is sometimes advocated for women, the kind Naomi advocates when she tells Ruth, in effect, "Don't say anything, just be attractive, do anything you can to make him want you." Ruth rejects that advice and speaks up when she has the opportunity. She has something to say, and she says it, revealing to Boaz a heart that is sensitive and obedient to the Word of God.

The Industrial Revolution of the late 18th and 19th centuries did a lot to separate the spheres of responsibility for men and women. In the pre-industrial world, couples and even entire families worked together in the same location, usually a farm or a shop. Practically all businesses were home-based businesses, so the spheres of men and women were close, and even overlapped.

Ruth and Boaz lived in the pre-industrial world of ancient Israel, and they worked in the same field, talked about the same issues, and articulated the same heart-felt hopes and dreams. They both talked about spiritual matters and the role of God in each other's lives. They both challenged each other to be aware of the Lord and obedient to His Word. Since both were made in God's image, they treated each other with respect and equality. Neither Boaz nor Ruth needed to demand equality or acceptance; it flowed naturally out of their hearts and their character, as they sought to be God's instrument of blessing in each other's life.

This is not to say that Ruth and Boaz have erased the God-given uniqueness of a man and a woman. They recognize that men and women are equal, but not the same. The things that Ruth talks about are different from the things Boaz talks about. They complement each other, and complete in each other what the other lacks and needs.

In Ruth 2:13, Ruth says, "You have spoken to my heart," a statement Boaz couldn't make at that point. Boaz couldn't evaluate what was happening in the relationship. He spoke about provision and protection for her, about his appreciation of her. He created an environment of confidence and safety for her. He cared about Ruth, because he saw her as a woman of excellence who trusted God—and he was quick to put a spotlight on her excellent qualities for all to see. He openly proclaimed her value for the onlookers to hear.

Later, in Ruth 3:11, Boaz tells Ruth, in effect, "You don't need to be afraid of the present or of the future." For years, Ruth and Naomi have been living with intense pain because of the past, and immense uncertainty and fear regarding the present and the future. Boaz understands Ruth's heart and now offers to shield her from the uncertainty and fear she has been living with for so long. Thus, Boaz makes it possible for Ruth to give him the gift of genuine heart-to-heart communication about their relationship. He talks about her needs, she talks about their needs.

As a result, Ruth who is able to say in verse 13, "You have given me comfort and have spoken to the heart of your servant. Because of your words, you and I are connected to one another at the heart. What you have done in speaking well of me and allowing me to be protected has penetrated my innermost being, my soul, my emotions, my spirit. You have built a bridge of deep understanding and communication." Ruth's statement of connectedness with Boaz is something Boaz desperately needs to hear.

Later, in chapter 3, Ruth speaks to Boaz out of a grateful realization of what God has created between them. There, on the threshing floor, she speaks of a covering—the covering of marriage. There is a beautiful cycle of intimacy suggested in the metaphor of the covering: The covering speaks of protection; a sense of protection and security enables two people to feel safe enough to be intimate, open, and transparent with each other; the more intimate and vulnerable two people are with each other, the more protection they give to each other, which leads to still greater intimacy, then still greater protection, in the perpetual cycle of a deepening, growing relationship.

Fresh water and poisonous water

James, the brother of Jesus, was a down-to-earth sort of a fellow who wrote the book of James in the New Testament. In James 3:10–11, he writes:

> Out of the same mouth come praise and cursing. My brothers, this should not be. Can both fresh water and salt water flow from the same spring?

In other words, if what is coming out of your mouth is brackish, it means that your heart is corrupt and deadly. You discover what's inside you by hearing what you say.

Often, people will do or say something very corrupt or hurtful or hateful, and later marvel at themselves, saying, "That was so out-of-character!" No, that was not out of character—it was a *revelation* of character. The mouth simply revealed something that was hidden in the heart. Instead of running from that revelation or rationalizing it, we need to face it squarely, confess it to God, and ask Him to remove that brackishness and foulness from our inner being.

We can apply this insight to relationships between men and women, to friendships, or to any other relationship. What we say displays who we are. If you've had a history of shallow relationships, if friendship after friendship begins in your life then quickly dies, then that is a revelation of something that is going on inside of you. If you're so afraid of life that you pull the covers over your head every time someone gets close, if relationships are so hard that you're afraid of them, you're saying something about what you believe about your own worthiness.

A person who speaks only of shallow, unimportant things is saying what they believe of themselves, and what they believe about God. If outbursts of anger and defensiveness wreck every relationship you've ever been in, then that is a revelation about something that's going on inside you. There's a brackish, poisonous spring erupting inside you, and only God can turn that bad water into something sweet, pure, and life-giving.

Keeping these truths in mind, consider for a moment the story of Jesus' encounter with the woman of Samaria in John 4. If you are looking for a woman in the Bible who is the complete polar opposite of Ruth, it is certainly this woman. She is an immoral woman who gives no thought for God's plan in her life. Yet it is also clear that this woman is truly seeking and searching. She has gone through a series of marriages and relationships, and none of them have satisfied her. She longs for the kind of caring, respectful, protective relationship that Ruth has found in Boaz—but she despairs of ever finding such love.

This woman comes to Jacob's well in the heat of the day because she can't come when the other women are there. She is an outcast, and the other women are threatened by her. She has no friends among the women in the town. The men in the town only use her. She is a Samaritan who has no business conversing with Jews. She is isolated by her social status and her low moral standards. She is a woman with whom the disciples are astonished to hear Jesus conversing.

All her life, the Samaritan woman has longed to find someone who would speak to her heart, someone who would care enough about her to value her, respect her, treat her as an equal, and say that she is good and valuable and worthy. She has had one man after another—five husbands—and now she is living out of wedlock, "shacking up" with a man who is not her husband. She longs for an emotional and spiritual connection, but she has nothing to draw on. There is nothing inside her that will produce it, and no one outside of her who will affirm her worth and speak to her heart.

Then, at Jacob's well, she encounters the Lord Jesus Christ.

There, Jesus makes a remarkable statement to her. He says in verse 10, "If you knew the gift of God and who it is that asks you for a drink, you would have asked him and he would have given you living water." In other words, "If you understood how much love I have for you, if you understood My authority and power to bring about a radical transformation in your life, you would have asked, and I would have given you living water. You would have been changed into a channel of blessing instead of an object of loathing and exploitation in your community. If you understood, you would have asked, and I would have given you everything you ever longed for—love, connection, meaning, value, affirmation, acceptance, belonging."

Jesus spoke the language of love, the language of the heart to this woman—and she eagerly responded and accepted the love He offered her. It is the same love that a man of Israel named Boaz had been raised in, the same love a woman of Moab named Ruth had discovered when she was grafted into the Jewish community and the Jewish faith. Boaz and Ruth spoke the language of the heart to each other, the same language Jesus spoke to you and me, the same language we must learn to speak to one another in our marriages, our families, our churches, our neighborhoods, and our world.

The people all around us are thirsting to hear the language of love, spoken from our hearts to theirs. Our loved ones and our mates long to hear the language of love from us on a daily basis. May God perform His miracle of transformation in our hearts, so that our speech will express God's goodness inside of us—a good spring of clear, living water rippling out from our lives, bringing life and love to the world around us.

CHAPTER 8

THE END AND
THE MEANS

Ruth 3

As we move into the new millennium, women are more confused than ever before about sexuality, roles, and relationships. A recent article in *USA Today* shows how that confusion has been compounded by women's magazines such as *Cosmopolitan*, *Ms.*, and *Glamour*. The covers of today's women's magazines, observes reporter Barbara Reynolds, "trumpet sex as sport, affairs as routine, or porn stars as celebrities." She goes on to say:

> Most women's mags have long used romance, love and family—and, inevitably, sex—as mainstays, but some now are pushing the limits of decency. They're becoming more tawdry and displaying women more as bodies, without souls or minds. If women accept these images of themselves, they are losing the battle against rape, domestic violence and sexual harassment. . . .
>
> Ads in women's mags and other periodicals also are busy playing the sex game. "Many of the ads are as close to pornographic as you can get. And just like the editorial content, some ads display women as helpless objects, having to look good and be sexually available for men," says ex-fashion model Ann Simonton of Media Watch in Santa Cruz, Calif.[1]

So on the one hand, women today are being bombarded with the dehumanizing message that they are sex objects, and that the only kind of relationship a man and a woman can have is a sexual relationship. In short, we are being sold the lie that the human mind, soul, and body exist merely to serve as a life-support system for the human genitalia.

On the other hand, many women today are being sold a message that comes from the opposite end of the spectrum—a romanticized, fairy-tale message that claims that for every woman there is a soulmate, a dream lover, a romantic fantasy destiny that is written in the stars. That is the premise of the hugely successful film, *Sleepless in Seattle*.

In that movie, a woman named Annie (Meg Ryan) falls in love with a man she's never met, a radio talk show host named Sam (Tom Hanks). Though she is on the verge of marrying a handsome, successful young businessman named Walter, she becomes obsessed when she hears Sam's voice on the radio. Annie believes that if they could meet, Sam would fall in love with her and they would live happily ever after. So she dumps her fiancé, hops in her car, and drives from Baltimore to Seattle to pursue this stranger on the radio.

Throughout the film, there are little vignettes which depict the stars in the heavens rearranging and realigning themselves to astrologically bring Sam and Annie together. Finally, when Sam and Annie meet for the first time, it is clear that they are soulmates. Their eyes lock on to each other, and there is magic in the air. According to *Sleepless in Seattle*, the perfect, just-right person for you is out there, waiting to be discovered. The name of your dream lover is written among the stars.

Both of these extremes are false. Human beings are not mere machines designed to perform the sex act as often as possible. But at the same time, we have to acknowledge that it is equally false to believe that human beings are characters in a fairy tale, magically brought together by the stars as a soundtrack of violins swells in the background.

Tragically, many people go through life experiencing lust, engaging in sex, but never finding *love*. They never experience a relationship that is any more profound than the relationship between a couple of stray dogs in heat. Equally tragic, many other people go through life vainly believing that "someday my prince will come." They go through relationship after relationship, looking for—and never finding—Prince Charming.

But here, in Ruth chapter 3, we discover God's plan for romantic love between a man and a woman—a relationship that includes sexuality, but goes far deeper than sex alone; a relationship that is magical in its richness and depth, but which is rooted in the reality of everyday living; a relationship in which a man and woman come together as real flesh-and-blood human beings, not as fantasy images from a fairy tale.

A beautiful, reciprocal relationship

If you open the first book of the New Testament, you will find these words—words which, unfortunately, many people pass over without much thought or close examination:

> A record of the genealogy of Jesus Christ the son of David, the son of Abraham:
>> Abraham was the father of Isaac,
>> Isaac the father of Jacob,
>> Jacob the father of Judah and his brothers,
>> Judah the father of Perez and Zerah,
>>> whose mother was Tamar,
>> Perez the father of Hezron,
>> Hezron the father of Ram,
>> Ram the father of Amminadab,
>> Amminadab the father of Nahshon,
>> Nahshon the father of Salmon,

> Salmon the father of Boaz,
>   whose mother was Rahab,
> Boaz the father of Obed,
>   whose mother was Ruth,
> Obed the father of Jesse,
> and Jesse the father of King David.
>
> (Matthew 1:1–6)

Many people who want to know Christ will begin with the book of Matthew. So they encounter Him first by meeting His family—the people God chose and prepared as the family tree for the Messiah. If you have carefully examined that list, then you've already noticed that two of the names on the Messiah's family tree are Boaz and Ruth.

Looking more closely, we see that Boaz was descended from Rahab—the Canaanite prostitute who helped Joshua and the children of Israel during the conquest of the Promised Land (see Joshua 2:1–3 and 6:17–23). But one of the striking features about Boaz, despite this heritage, is his easy and natural manliness. He stands as an impressive, instructive example of what it truly means to be a man. Unlike so many men today, Boaz is not domineering or overbearing, nor is he withdrawn or uncertain of himself. He commands without lording it over others, he is assertive without being aggressive, he is confident without being arrogant.

And what is Ruth like? Even amid the dust and sweat of her labor, she maintains a beautiful, pleasing aura of femininity about her. She appreciates, honors, and encourages Boaz. She knows how to be attractive yet modest, humble yet dignified, gracious and grateful without resorting to empty flattery.

Here are two people whose egos are neither over-large nor stunted. They are comfortable and not self-conscious within their own skin, within their own souls, within their own sexuality. They respect themselves and others. The beginning of their love relationship is utterly reciprocal—she does not chase or manipulate him, he does not chase or manipulate her. They come together, mutually and beautifully.

The end of Ruth chapter 2 records that, in the days following their meeting, Ruth (and presumably Boaz) continued to spend their time harvesting in the fields. It is easy to believe that as the days went by, they began to care for each other and appreciate each other. Their attraction for each other grew—not the completely animal-like, sexual attraction that so many people settle for today, nor the fantasy attraction that is rooted in the unrealistic romanticism of fairy tales and romance novels. The love that grew between Ruth and Boaz was rooted in a clear-eyed, realistic respect and awareness of the inner reality of each other. Boaz was attracted to the beautiful, sweet, humble character of Ruth, and Ruth was attracted to the strong, caring, Christlike character of Boaz. As their mutual attraction grew, they approached an important turning point in their relationship.

The revolution of rising expectations

Boaz and Ruth each loved God and lived by faith in God, trusting their Heavenly Father to provide for them. And it appeared that God had blessed them far beyond their wildest hopes and dreams. But in Ruth chapter 3, Boaz and Ruth entered a stage in their relationship that sociologists call "the revolution of rising expectations." It is possible for an individual, a family, or a nation to live under difficult circumstances for a long period of time, as Ruth and Naomi had for ten years. But once hope arises that those circumstances might soon change for the better, the situation quickly becomes unbearable.

C. S. Lewis wrote of the experience he and his wife, Joy, went through during her bout with cancer. When the cancer was first diagnosed, the doctors offered no hope. They expected her to die within months, and that was that. So Lewis and his wife prepared themselves for the end. But then the cancer went into remission, and for a while it seemed that she had been healed. They began to think about the future, and to make plans and dream dreams together. Months later, when the cancer returned once more, the recurrence of the cancer was much more emotionally devastating for both of them than the original onset had been. They had received an injection of hope—a "revolution of rising expectations"—and when their hopes fell through, their faith was dealt a heavy blow. Though their faith triumphed in the end, they had to first pass through the shadowlands of doubt and despair.

Amid different circumstances but in a parallel way, Ruth and Boaz go through a similar experience of hopes raised—then shaken. They did not expect to fall in love. Both Ruth and Boaz had learned to trust God for their daily lives, never expecting that God would bring the wonder and excitement of romantic love into their lives again. But now that they had found each other, now that their hopes were raised, now that they were about to think about the future, to make plans and dream dreams together, Ruth and Boaz suddenly found it much more difficult to trust God.

Their situation is not helped by Ruth's scheming mother-in-law, Naomi, a servant of the flesh, who adds to their temptation by prodding Ruth and Boaz to get ahead of God and act on their feelings rather than acting out of obedience to the will of God. In Ruth 3:1–5, we find Naomi plotting to throw Ruth and Boaz together, little realizing that if she gets her way, she will actually *undermine* God's plan to unite them in His own way, in His own time:

> One day Naomi her mother-in-law said to her, "My daughter, should I not try to find a home for you, where you will be well provided for? Is not Boaz, with whose

servant girls you have been, a kinsman of ours? Tonight he will be winnowing barley on the threshing floor. Wash and perfume yourself, and put on your best clothes. Then go down to the threshing floor, but don't let him know you are there until he has finished eating and drinking. When he lies down, note the place where he is lying. Then go and uncover his feet and lie down. He will tell you what to do."

"I will do whatever you say," Ruth answered.

We would have to be fairly naive not to understand what Naomi is suggesting at this point. She is saying, in effect, "Ruth, make yourself as physically attractive as you possibly can. Wash yourself, anoint yourself, dress in your best clothes and then, when Boaz is most vulnerable, when he has eaten and drank and his defenses are down, snuggle up next to him—and let human nature take its course." We can almost detect a knowing wink on Naomi's face.

We can say this for Naomi: She has correctly assessed the situation. Two harvests have taken place since Ruth and Boaz first met one another, so it is high time that Ruth and Boaz clarify the precise nature of their relationship. And, to be fair to Naomi, she was absolutely justified in wanting to help Ruth find security and a home. As a poor woman, a foreigner, a widow, Ruth's situation in Israel was very precarious. Naomi genuinely cared about Ruth's future welfare and security—and in her own bumbling way, she was trying to help.

But I think it's fair to suspect that Naomi's motives for helping Ruth may well have had a selfish component as well. Recognizing that Ruth is committed to taking care of her, Naomi is quick to grasp the fact that any advantages for Ruth are also advantages for Naomi. If Ruth is well taken care of, then Naomi will be, too.

At this point, we can be sure Boaz and Ruth are in love and want to marry each other. Clearly, Naomi wants them to get married. As we shall see, everyone around them wants them to get married; there will be a great crescendo of joy when their marriage takes place. Most of all God wants them to get married. But the question is: By what means will this marriage come about? By God's means—or human means?

Boaz and Naomi have a positive, righteous goal in mind, and their intentions are perfectly honorable. But Naomi attempts to use human wiles to achieve that good goal. Naomi's starting point is, "We can't trust God—so let me take over! I will provide security for you, Ruth!" She thinks she needs to step in and shape events before a golden opportunity is lost.

Naomi tells Ruth, in effect, "Boaz will be at a harvest party tonight, after the threshing takes place [the conclusion of the threshing was typically a festival time]. He'll go to sleep outside with the grain that's been harvested. Ruth, make yourself as attractive as you can. Bathe and put on a fragrance, and adorn yourself in your nicest clothes. Wait until he has eaten and drunk as much as he's going to." In verse 6, we will see that Boaz is "in good spirits" after eating and drinking, so he was, perhaps, a bit tipsy from the wine. "When it's dark," Naomi continues, "get close to him and make your move."

Nowhere in this plan does Naomi make any reference to God's involvement. She simply directs Ruth to wait until Boaz's defenses are down, then beguile him with her feminine allure. Is Naomi really prodding Ruth to seduce Boaz, committing sexual sin on the threshing floor? Whether or not Naomi is capable of such a suggestion, we can be sure that Ruth would never agree to such a plan.

I suspect that what Naomi has in mind is for Ruth to merely waft her scent in his direction, and hope that he would simply be captivated by her presence. Certainly, Naomi intended that Ruth should seduce Boaz—but whether she intended that Ruth should offer herself sexually or merely seduce him emotionally is not entirely clear. Personally, I believe Naomi wants Ruth to beguile Boaz, not seduce him. At the very least, she intends that the evening will be charged with enough sexual tension to lure Boaz into a decision based on the power of romantic possibilities. In verses 6–13, we see what happens next:

> So she went down to the threshing floor and did everything her mother-in-law told her to do.
>
> When Boaz had finished eating and drinking and was in good spirits, he went over to lie down at the far end of the grain pile. Ruth approached quietly, uncovered his feet and lay down. In the middle of the night something startled the man, and he turned and discovered a woman lying at his feet.
>
> "Who are you?" he asked.
>
> "I am your servant Ruth," she said. "Spread the corner of your garment over me, since you are a kinsman-redeemer."
>
> "The LORD bless you, my daughter," he replied. "This kindness is greater than that which you showed earlier: You have not run after the younger men, whether rich or poor. And now, my daughter, don't be afraid. I will do for you all you ask. All my fellow townsmen know that you are a woman of noble character. Although it is true that I am near of kin, there is a kinsman-redeemer nearer than I. Stay here for the night, and in the morning if he wants to redeem, good; let him redeem. But if he is not willing, as surely as the LORD lives I will do it. Lie here until morning."

It is not clear why Ruth went along with Naomi's plan as far as she did. Perhaps it was out of respect for her mother-in-law. But it is clear, as the story unfolds, that Ruth has not bought Naomi's complete program. She has no intention of carrying out Naomi's scheme and seducing Boaz, which would be a manipulative, unrighteous act.

So when Boaz awakes and realizes that a woman is at his feet, he begins to question her. Instead of snuggling up to him and seducing him while his defenses are down, Ruth reminds him of Scripture. In so doing, she makes it clear to Boaz that she has no dishonorable intentions, while at the same time she appeals to a responsibility he has under the law of God.

Naomi's plan versus God's plan

In Deuteronomy 25, there is a provision in the Law that if a man dies without a son to inherit his property, then his brother or another close relative (from the Latin *levir* "brother-in-law") has a responsibility to marry the widow and father a child to bear the name of the deceased man and inherit his property. A related provision of the Law holds that if a widow must sell property in order to survive, then a *go'el* or kinsman-redeemer must step in and buy back the property for her and her family in order to maintain the family inheritance. If there is no *go'el* or kinsman-redeemer, then the family might lose the family property forever, and could even be forced to sell themselves into slavery in order to survive. That is a very foreign-sounding concept to us, but it made much more sense in a tribal culture that was tied to the gift of the Promised Land. To the people of Israel, property was crucial to their sense of nationhood, so it was crucially important to continue the family name, generation after generation.

These practices originate with God, and they tell us something about the character of God. He makes provision for daily bread. He provides a way to relieve the tragedy of the past, and pay the price to buy a slave's freedom. He also provides a secure home for the future even when death intervenes. All of these things point to spiritual realities in Christ. God is the one whose power gives us what we need each day. He is the one who has bought us and redeemed us out of slavery to sin, and He is the one in whom we hope for the future.

Even before the birth of Christ, God's people were taught by the law of God that He was deeply committed to meeting their needs. It was on that basis that Ruth acted in faith. If the Lord cared enough about her to give these laws and touch her heart, then she knew she could trust Him to care for her, provide for her future, and reward her faith.

In verse 9, after Boaz awakens and asks, "Who are you?" Ruth replies, "I am your servant Ruth. Spread the corner of your garment over me, since you are a kinsman-redeemer." In other words, Ruth is saying, "My husband died without an heir, so you, as his kinsman, have a responsibility before God to protect me and to provide him an heir." She is appealing to Boaz's responsibility before God, not appealing to his sexuality. Ruth understands what so many people today have forgotten: We are more than mere sexual animals, to be led about and manipulated by our passions. We are also spiritual beings, and Ruth treats Boaz with the respect that a spiritual being deserves. Instead of nibbling his ear and seducing him, as Naomi planned, Ruth appeals to his sense of honor and godly responsibility.

Ruth's choice of words is significant: "Spread the corner of your garment over me." There are other places in the Old Testament where that phrase is a description of marriage. The idiom sometimes conveys the idea of spreading wings over someone, the way a mother bird spreads its wings to protect a baby bird. It is similar to the phrase Boaz used in Ruth 2:12, when he referred to the fact that Ruth had sought refuge under the wings of the God of Israel.

In her quiet, respectful way, Ruth is saying to Boaz, "Please marry me, please protect me," and the basis of her request is not romantic attraction but the Law of God. It is clear in this passage that Ruth and Boaz see themselves as servants of God in each other's lives. Naomi's plan would have brought Ruth and Boaz down into sin. But Ruth's godly actions elevate herself and Boaz in a spiritual way, resulting in greater obedience and stronger faith.

After Ruth speaks to Boaz of his responsibility, Boaz responds with a beautiful word of encouragement and gratitude (verse 10): "The LORD bless you, my daughter. This kindness is greater than that which you showed earlier: You have not run after the younger men, whether rich or poor." In other words, "Thank you for not going after young men. The caring you have shown for me is a great honor."

But now a problem arises. True to her character, Ruth has followed God's plan and maintained godly morality. She trusted in her Lord, not her feminine wiles. But in doing so, she comes to a moment of crisis: By following the Law of God, she may end up losing Boaz!

The problem is simply this: Though Boaz is in line to marry Ruth and be her kinsman-redeemer, he is not *first* in line—there is *another* kinsman who is closer to Ruth than Boaz. So Boaz essentially tells her, "Unfortunately, there is another man who ought to face this responsibility and meet your need for a husband. If we are going to make decisions in line with the LORD's will, we will first have to give this man the opportunity to accept his responsibility."

Imagine Ruth's emotions at this point! She has come so far, endured so much, and her hopes have been raised so high—only to discover that she might lose the man she loves. It would be so easy to simply follow Naomi's advice, seduce Boaz, and make him take responsibility for her. It would be so easy to simply short-circuit God's will and make sure that Ruth ends up with Boaz instead of this other man. After all, God brought Ruth and Boaz together, so He surely must want them to be together. What would be the harm of making a little short-cut in God's plan and helping things along?

That is the temptation we yield to so readily today—the temptation to say, "The end justifies the means." It's easy for us to want something that is good, something that is valuable, something everyone around us agrees is good—but to go about the wrong way. There's nothing at all wrong with wanting that relationship, that new job, that new ministry, that new car or house or computer—but are we trusting God and working within His timing and will, or are we trying to hurry His plan along with a little underhandedness of our own?

We see this problem a lot in what I would call "Christian hucksterism," which often involves well-intentioned people trying to do God's will through human manipulation. Sometimes people are so determined to see the gospel spread and the church grow that they use pressure tactics, false promises, phony come-ons, and outright lies to yank people into the kingdom. They are so anxious to achieve a good end that they will resort to any means (including sinful, deceptive means) to achieve it.

Marriages, too, often run into problems with this attitude that "the end justifies the means." For example: "My husband doesn't know what's good for him—but I do. So I'll just twist his arm until he goes to church with me." Or, "I know my wife has been leery of ocean trips ever since she saw the movie *Titanic*, but I'll just keep badgering her, because I know she'd really love an Alaskan cruise, once she was on the ship."

Sometimes our end-justifies-the-means deceptions can seem so innocent. "I didn't actually lie to the boss. He thinks the Acme Industries deal was my idea—and since I'm getting a promotion, why should I correct his mistaken impression?"

But Ruth and Boaz refused to yield to the false and deceptive notion that the end justifies the means. God holds us accountable for the means we use, and He expects us to trust Him to accomplish His ends. That is what Ruth and Boaz did—trusting that He was faithful to complete what He had begun in their lives. God had been faithful to them up to that point, so they ignored the manipulative schemes of Naomi and chose to continue doing what was right.

Sexual attraction and moral choices

Though Aurelius Augustinius was born some 1,600 years ago, he had a lifestyle and an outlook on life that is exactly like that of the people around us today. A rebellious teenager, he had his first sexual encounter at age 16, and went on to live a wild, promiscuous lifestyle. His thinking was dominated by thoughts of sex, and he was continually on the prowl for his next sexual conquest. He recognized his lifestyle as one of out-and-out sin, and he didn't care—in fact he proudly claimed he enjoyed sinning!

In his twenties, young Aurelius began living with a woman in an unmarried state, and they soon became the unwed parents of a young son. Rejecting his responsibilities as a father, and not wanting to be tied down, he abandoned the woman and the child. He was perplexed that his hedonistic, sex-drenched lifestyle didn't satisfy, and he began studying various philosophies in search of the meaning of life. He delved into astrology and the occult, hoping to find the satisfaction he was missing. He later reflected on those "wasted years," recalling, "I was led astray, and I led others astray, deceived and deceiving in all manner of lusts."

In his mid-thirties, Aurelius experienced a dramatic conversion to Jesus Christ, yet even after his conversion and baptism he was tormented by sexual temptation. His prayer expressed the inner conflict he felt: "Lord, make me chaste—but not yet." Finally, through the counsel of some mature Christian friends, he learned the secret of inner peace: He needed to let God be Lord of his life, including his sex life and his thought life. He needed to allow God alone to be his joy. "This is the blessed life," he later wrote in a psalm to God, "to rejoice in You, to You, on account of You, this and nothing else. Those who think it other than this pursue another joy, which is not true joy."

Today, Aurelius is known by another name: St. Augustine.

The conduct of Boaz and Ruth in Ruth 3 indicates that they already understood the lesson that Aurelius Augustine learned the hard way: The way to respond to difficult moral choices and sexual temptation is by letting God have first place in every corner of your life.

As we examine Ruth chapter 3 with our sanctified imaginations, seeking to read the subtleties of the story, we sense a few important facets of the budding relationship between Boaz and Ruth. First, they have been working together for a while. Ruth has been gleaning, and Boaz has been overseeing the work of his harvesters. They have probably seen one another day after day. This has gone on for two months, through two harvests, and they clearly have feelings for one another.

But there are barriers which stand in the way of Ruth and Boaz having a life together. One barrier is the fact that Ruth feels unworthy of Boaz (she expressed these feelings in chapter 2 when she asked Boaz, "Why would you even notice me?" (see verse 10) and, "I'm not even worthy to work for you" (see verse 13). Another barrier is the fact that Boaz apparently considers himself too old for her (see 3:10). And the most important barrier of all is a legal barrier: Boaz is aware of another kinsman with a stronger claim to marry Ruth—a kinsman Naomi and Ruth might not even know about.

Naomi proceeds to try to knock down all these barriers by throwing Ruth and Boaz together in the grain barn in the middle of the night. So Naomi proceeds to set these events in motion.

Notice that Ruth chapter 2 and chapter 3 have the same structure. They both begin with a conversation between Ruth and Naomi. Then Ruth goes off to the place of work, either the field or the threshing floor. She and Boaz have a conversation, and she comes back with food. In both cases, Boaz doesn't recognize Ruth at first (compare 2:5 with 3:9). Then, in each case, when he discovers who she is, he finds out a great deal more than he expected. These are important parallels.

But there are significant differences between these chapters, too. In chapter 2, Ruth just "happens" onto the field of Boaz, whereas in chapter 3, Naomi carefully sets up the encounter between the two lovers. In chapter 2, the couple is surrounded by other people, and the scene takes place in broad daylight. In chapter 3, however, Ruth and Boaz are alone at night, in a setting of obvious sexual tension and temptation.

Naomi's plan is for Ruth to beguile Boaz, and to ingratiate herself with him. In essence, Naomi wants Ruth to maneuver and manipulate Boaz. The problem is that you can't achieve the purposes of God by maneuvering and manipulating people against their better judgment. You can't create a relationship of honesty and depth out of deception and the surface feelings of sexual tension. Crafty, stealthy schemes are not the stuff out of which healthy relationships are made.

It is interesting to note that while Ruth did as Naomi instructed, she clearly did so for different reasons than Naomi's reasons. She was a godly young woman who respected and honored her mother-in-law, which she did in obedience to the scriptural command to "honor your father and mother." Naomi was, by marriage, Ruth's mother, and she was wise enough to do as she was told by her mother—but not for the reason that Naomi gave her, which was an unrighteous reason. (Honoring parents, obviously, does not include obeying parental dictates that violate the Scriptures.)

As Ruth prepared for the evening, bathing and applying fragrance and putting on her best clothes, her thoughts must have turned to questions about God's purposes and the evidence of Boaz's commitment to righteousness. Understanding the implications of what Naomi had instructed her to do, she might have prayed, "Lord, Boaz is not the kind of man Naomi assumes him to be. How can I honor Naomi—and still trust and obey Your will during this night? Please show me what to do!"

And the Lord clearly did show Ruth what to do. Perhaps her voice quavered as she spoke to Boaz about a responsibility based on the teaching of Scripture. In any case, her words to Boaz were, in effect, "As a kinsman, please be my *go'el*; as my *levir*, be my kinsman-redeemer. Please cover me with the protection of marriage." Ruth's literal words in verse 9 are, "I am your servant Ruth. Spread the corner of your garment over me, since you are a kinsman-redeemer."

This expression, "spread the corner of your garment over me," unquestionably refers to marriage, not the blanket which covers Boaz. The added clause, "since you are my kinsman-redeemer," makes this clear. To this day, Jews in many parts of the world get married under a canopy, which is symbolic of the covering of marriage that Ruth speaks of here. In Ezekiel 16, the same language is used when God draws near to Israel, his fallen young bride, and initiates a marriage relationship with her.

Ruth declares that Boaz should marry her because he has a responsibility from God as a kinsman. Elimelech is dead and Mahlon is dead, and there is property that will be lost, a family name that will never be known of again. It was the clear responsibility of the family members to protect the property and provide an heir. Ruth appeals to Boaz to do what is right before the Lord.

Such a request fit Boaz exactly, since he lived his life as an instrument of God's blessing in the lives of others. Now Ruth offers him the opportunity to become the agent of protection that she has sought from the Lord. No doubt, Boaz would have been eager to marry a beautiful young woman like Ruth, but held back from asking her, thinking himself too old for her. In his typical selfless thinking, he might have told himself, "She would never want to be tied down to an old codger like me!" So Naomi completely misjudged Boaz. Her idea of trying to entice Boaz with feminine wiles wouldn't have worked—Boaz was too unselfish, too much a godly gentleman, to act on the basis of sexual attraction alone.

With a heart sensitive to the leading of the Holy Spirit, Ruth understood Boaz and his motivations. She knew better than to appeal to his sexuality; she appealed instead to his spirituality and his sense of responsibility.

A marriage relationship functions properly and provides security when both husband and wife can speak to each other as honestly and as spiritually as Ruth spoke to Boaz. A godly spouse will speak to you of the things of God and will remind you of who you are before God. A godly spouse will not seek to manipulate you sexually, but will draw out the best in you spiritually. A godly spouse will help you believe in you when you can't believe in yourself, and will strengthen you in the obedience your heart longs for.

In the end, what actually takes place between Ruth and Boaz on the threshing floor has nothing to do with Ruth's clothing or her fragrance or how much wine Boaz might have consumed. Not one of the things that Naomi mentions as being key factors even comes into play. Instead, it is Ruth's godliness and the purity of her spirit—so sensitively attuned to the Spirit of God—that is the deciding factor.

Boaz responds by blessing Ruth, telling her, in effect, "May you be blessed of the LORD. Don't be afraid. God will act to protect you—and so will I." In the process, Boaz discovers (thanks to Ruth's courageous statement) that he is not, as he supposed, too old for her to be interested in him. In contradiction of Naomi's schemes, the evening has not become one of sexual tension leading to reckless decision-making, but an opportunity for two people to pray for each other, to speak of God to each other, to see boundaries come down. In the process, God's will is accomplished in a beautiful way.

Many Christians today find it difficult to resist sexual temptation. Like young St. Augustine, our prayer is, "Lord, make me chaste, make me pure—but not quite yet." We are caught in the struggle between our sexual nature and our spiritual nature, between wanting to do what *feels* good versus wanting to do what *is* good. Our sex-drenched, immoral culture hammers away at us, urging us to do what is wrong, just as Naomi urged Ruth. This is a struggle for young Christians with racing hormones, of course—but it is also a struggle for middle-aged and older Christians as well. It is a struggle for the married and the unmarried. There are so many temptations—youthful fornication, adultery, pornography, phone sex, cybersex, and more. But God wants our focus to be in Him, not in these sordid and sinful behaviors.

It is often easy for us to rationalize sexual sin. It is easy for two Christian lovers to say to themselves, "We're going to get married in a few months anyway—it's almost as if we're married now. If we're careful, if we make sure no pregnancy occurs, what would be the harm?" But there is *always* harm when we step outside of God's perfect will, and ahead of His perfect timing for our lives. We need to observe the lesson the life of Ruth teaches us. She refused to take any short-cuts in her relationship with Boaz. She patiently listened to God and followed His plan, not the plan of Naomi, not the will of human flesh. And, as we will see in Ruth chapter 4, she is rewarded for her obedience beyond her wildest dreams of joy and romance.

Clearly, the decision to live by faith always entails risk. Neither Boaz nor Ruth had any guarantee that they would end up together—but they were willing to risk their relationship, their future together, on the promises and character of God. Imagine what that night was like. Ruth lay at Boaz's feet until just before dawn, but we don't know if either of them slept. Did they whisper to one another, or pray together to the Lord? Did they gaze at the stars and dream of the future? We don't know, but we do know that they spent the night very close to one another, unsure of whether they would ever be so close again.

The Christian life is mirrored in the story of Ruth and Boaz. The book of Hebrews says that those who put their faith in God are strangers in a strange land, sojourners in a foreign country. The life of a stranger in a foreign land is a risky life. We can choose to retreat from the risk of faith as Naomi did, attempting to find security by steering events and engineering outcomes for ourselves. Or we can choose to live like Ruth, taking risks of faith, trusting that God will be true to His promises and His character.

What will we choose—to live like Naomi or to live like Ruth? I trust and pray that, in your life and mine, there can only be one answer to that question.

A woman of excellence

Before we leave Ruth chapter 3, notice again the words of Boaz to Ruth in verse 10: "The LORD bless you, my daughter. This kindness is greater than that which you showed earlier: You have not run after the younger men, whether rich or poor." It is important to see that he is not primarily taken by her beauty—although he acknowledges her attractiveness when he says that she could have had a younger man and found a home and security that way. What he truly says to her is this: "You are a woman of excellence on the inside. You have placed yourself under the protection of God, and you have a kind and godly spirit. You love God and His purposes first. You are somebody who has been renewed on the inside. And that is why you have captured my heart—not your outer beauty, but your holiness and the beauty of your character."

The rest of the night passes, and Boaz is concerned to make sure that her reputation isn't ruined, that no one should misunderstand what has happened. So Boaz sends Ruth back home before dawn so that no one will recognize her. He also gives her enough grain to encourage her mother-in-law— who, of course, pays close attention to such things!

The next day, Boaz goes into the town. The text doesn't tell us exactly how Boaz is related to the family of Elimelech, but it does tell us that there is someone in town who is a nearer relative to Elimelech than Boaz. It is this other man who, by God's law, should accept the responsibility as the *go'el* and the *levir* ahead of Boaz.

So Boaz is determined to speak to that man and settle the matter. This conversation will take place at the city gate.

CHAPTER 9

THE INFINITE/
INTIMATE GOD

Ruth 4

As scientists amass information about the universe we live in, it becomes more and more difficult to believe that time and space, matter and energy have always existed. With each new discovery, the discussion of the beginning and end of the universe increasingly becomes a discussion of spiritual things, even among agnostics and atheists.

Stephen Hawking, the wheelchair-bound mathematician who is widely considered the equal of Einstein, puts it this way: "The odds against a universe like ours emerging out of something like the Big Bang are enormous. I think there are clearly religious implications whenever you start to discuss the origins of the universe. There must be religious overtones".[1]

Leonard Shlain says today's physicists describe the Big Bang as "a hyper-expanding fireball containing light, space, time, energy, and matter. [The physicists'] simulation bears an uncanny similarity to the biblical story of Genesis. The creation of *light* was God's first act. Then He divided night from day *(time)*. Then He separated the firmament from the waters and land *(space)*. He then made the 'things' in the world *(matter)* and finally set them in motion *(energy)*. The computer-generated beginnings of the universe mirror the Bible's cosmology"[2] .

And Physicist Paul Davies puts the case this way in *God and the New Physics*[3]: "If the universe is simply an accident, the odds against it containing any appreciable order are ludicrously small. . . . There surely had to be a *selector* or *designer*" (emphasis in the original).

As our world rolls into the third millennium of the Christian era, scientists are beginning to agree with the Bible: Our universe exists as it does because an all-powerful intelligent Creator *willed* it to exist and *caused* it to exist.

Infinite—and intimate

At this point, you may be thinking, "That's very well and good—but what does the creation of the universe have to do with the story of Ruth and Boaz?" Well, it is important that we don't think of God *only* as a great, omnipotent, omniscient Creator. The Bible is our vital link between the two most amazing aspects of God: (1) He is vast, wise, and powerful beyond our comprehension; and (2) He is intimately, personally involved in our lives.

God is infinite—and intimate. The same God who created the universe out of nothing, who fashioned the subatomic particles out of pure logic, also cared enough to direct the lives of Naomi, Ruth, and Boaz. He cared enough to bring Ruth and Boaz together in a love relationship, a marriage relationship, that would place them in the ancestral line of the Messiah Himself, Jesus Christ.

The gospel of John shows us this same linkage between the infinite aspect of God and the intimate aspect of God. John chapter 1 opens with these words:

> In the beginning was the Word, and the Word was with God, and the Word was God. He was with God in the beginning.

Through him all things were made; without him nothing was made that has been made. In him was life, and that life was the light of men. (1:1–4)

Here we see the same omnipotent Being involved in the creation of the universe—and in the lives of human beings. This Being, God, was so involved with our human condition that, as John tells us, "The Word became flesh and made his dwelling among us" (1:14). Our Lord Jesus, the second person of the Trinity, was there in the beginning, at the explosion of the Big Bang. He spoke the universe into existence—and He became a human baby, grew to be a man, and died upon a wooden cross, suspended in time and space upon a rugged hill outside of the city of Jerusalem in Israel.

How can our finite minds possibly grasp the wonder and contradiction of that fact—that the Creator of the universe entered into His universe and allowed Himself to be put to death upon a tiny little patch of that universe? It staggers the imagination!

Jesus Christ was fully God, yet He became fully human. He walked in the same dust we walk in. He understood the same fears we feel. He entered into the same pain we experience. He identified with us completely in order that He might redeem us from our sin.

The Word of God would be a grand, exalted document if it spoke only of creation—but creation is only the beginning. God went on to do something even more amazing than the original creation: He produced the *new creation*—the redemption of miserable, pain-wracked, guilt-ridden, sin-infested human beings like you and me. The most astounding handiwork of God is not the indescribably complex universe He has created, but the transformation He has produced in the lives of ordinary people like you and me—and in the lives of people like Naomi, Ruth, and Boaz.

Boaz confronts the other kinsman

Returning to the book of Ruth, chapter 4, we see the hand of the Creator moving mightily in the lives of these three people, performing a subtle yet creative work. In the next few verses, we will see Him establish hope where there was no hope, bringing joy out of tremendous sorrow, meeting the needs of two impoverished widows, and transforming three lonely lives into a family. It begins with a bold, public act by Boaz at the town gate:

> Meanwhile Boaz went up to the town gate and sat there. When the kinsman-redeemer he had mentioned came along, Boaz said, "Come over here, my friend, and sit down." So he went over and sat down.
>
> Boaz took ten of the elders of the town and said, "Sit here," and they did so. Then he said to the kinsman-redeemer, "Naomi, who has come back from Moab, is selling the piece of land that belonged to our brother Elimelech. I thought I should bring the matter to your attention and suggest that you buy it in the presence of these seated here and in the presence of the elders of my people. If you will redeem it, do so. But if you will not, tell me, so I will know. For no one has the right to do it except you, and I am next in line."
>
> "I will redeem it," he said.
>
> Then Boaz said, "On the day you buy the land from Naomi and from Ruth the Moabitess, you acquire the dead man's widow, in order to maintain the name of the dead with his property."
>
> At this, the kinsman-redeemer said, "Then I cannot redeem it because I might endanger my own estate. You redeem it yourself. I cannot do it."
>
> (Now in earlier times in Israel, for the redemption and transfer of property to become final, one party took off his sandal and gave it to the other. This was the method of legalizing transactions in Israel.)

So the kinsman-redeemer said to Boaz, "Buy it yourself." And he removed his sandal.

Then Boaz announced to the elders and all the people, "Today you are witnesses that I have bought from Naomi all the property of Elimelech, Kilion and Mahlon. I have also acquired Ruth the Moabitess, Mahlon's widow, as my wife, in order to maintain the name of the dead with his property, so that his name will not disappear from among his family or from the town records. Today you are witnesses!"

Then the elders and all those at the gate said, "We are witnesses. May the LORD make the woman who is coming into your home like Rachel and Leah, who together built up the house of Israel. May you have standing in Ephrathah and be famous in Bethlehem. Through the offspring the LORD gives you by this young woman, may your family be like that of Perez, whom Tamar bore to Judah."

Boaz is a man of direct, straightforward action. In contrast to manipulative, behind-the-scenes schemers like Naomi, Boaz conducts his business out in the open where everyone can see. There are no hidden agendas, no sneaky plots with Boaz. Not only does he conduct his business in the open where the public can see, he goes out of his way to make sure there are plenty of eyewitnesses. First, he takes the kinsman aside and says, "Wait here," then he goes and collects the ten most trusted elders in town to serve as witnesses. He doesn't want anyone to be able to say he tricked this kinsman. Everything is going to be open and aboveboard.

Next, in front of the elders of the town, Boaz approaches this closest relative and says, in effect, "Naomi is a poor woman. She is finally to the point where she has to sell her family's property. Will you buy it?"

Remember, Naomi had been gone for ten years, and she and Ruth have come back poor, widowed, and without protection. We don't know exactly what has happened on Elimelech's land since the end of the famine. Most likely, Naomi and Elimelech leased the property or borrowed against it during the famine years, so that another person was farming it and reaping its produce. That would explain why a redeemer would need to, in effect, pay off the mortgage and redeem the property so that it could be retained in Elimelech's family.

Clearly, Naomi does not have the strength or resources to farm it herself, nor the money to redeem it. She has no standing or power to assert her right to property anymore. She is a poor, elderly widow—and few people in ancient Israel had less power than the poor, the elderly, and the widowed. Unable to fight for what is hers, she must relinquish her rights to this field.

So Boaz says to the near kinsman, "We need to stand up for Naomi because we're relatives, we're kinsman redeemers. We need to save the property for her." The other man thinks, "Terrific! I'll add a little to my own acreage. She's a widow getting on in years. Eventually, I'll get the land for myself."

But Boaz reminds him, "No, that really isn't the point. You're not allowed to add this property to your own. It belongs to the heirs of Elimelech. And remember, Elimelech had a son, Mahlon, who has also left a widow behind to be cared for. You're going to have to take care of two widows, and you have the responsibility to marry the young one and have a child who will inherit Mahlon's and Elimelech's name and property."

Now the other man begins to reconsider. He already has one wife and family, and he begins to think that two wives might be one wife too many! "This won't help my situation at all!" he thinks. "Who knows what jeopardy this will put my own children and my own inheritance in? No thanks— I'll pass."

So with the town elders as his witnesses, Boaz is free to redeem the property—and free to marry Ruth. Turning to the elders and any other men who are around the town gate at that time he says, "You are witnesses today that I have bought from the hand of Naomi all that belonged to Elimelech, Kilion, and Mahlon. Most of all, I now have the right to make Ruth, Mahlon's widow, my wife. I will raise up the name of these dead men, so that their line of ancestry and their good names will not be forgotten."

And the elders and the other men of the town reply, "We are witnesses."

And then these men say something very prophetic: "May God make the woman who is coming into your home—Ruth—like Rachel and Leah, who became mothers to the entire house of Israel." Indeed, as we will see, the descendants of Ruth shall write many more important chapters in the history of the house of Israel, for her descendants will include King David, King Solomon, and the King of Kings, the Messiah of Israel, Jesus of Nazareth.

Culture and character

There are cultural nuances in this story that bear a closer look—customs that are crucial to the story, even though they are unfamiliar to us today. First, there is the importance of family lines. Remember the history of the people of God: There were two important marks that were to distinguish the Israelites from the rest of the people of the world. Those of Abraham's line—the descendants of Isaac, the descendants of Jacob, the descendants of Jacob's twelve sons who fanned out across the Holy Land and beyond—were heirs of the special promises of God. So it was critically important that family lines be maintained and remembered.

Second, there is the importance of land. At the time of Moses and the Exodus, God led His people out of captivity in Egypt and into the land of promise. The promised land, Israel, continues to be the focus of history and international affairs today. This particular plot of land was to be the land of the Jews, and it will continue to be the focus of history on into the future, when the events of the book of Revelation unfold. The people of Israel were very conscious of their real estate, and what it meant to their family and to their Jewish society.

Third, there is the importance of the Law. Provision was made in the Law for protecting families and their descendants, even in situations of catastrophe and loss. According to the Law, the land was to be preserved as a family heritage, not sold or passed into the hands of others. When Boaz speaks to the responsible relative, he raises these issues—the issues of family lineage, land, and the Law. The land of Elimelech is under threat of loss. It must be sold, and this threatens the continuance of the dead man's family line. If Elimelech's kinsmen do not act responsibly according to the Law, Elimelech's family line will die out—a great tragedy in that culture.

Fourth, there is the matter of how official business was conducted in that culture. There were no courthouses, no notary publics, no deeds recorded in the county clerk's office, no file cabinets or computerized records. Official actions and transactions were established in the presence of reliable witnesses, and recorded in the minds and memories of those witnesses. If the elders of the town made a decision, that decision stood; if they witnessed an action between two citizens, it was as officially signed, sealed, and delivered as a legally signed and notarized contract would be today. Actions such as removing the sandal and handing it to the other party in the bargain lent an added air of ceremony and solemnity to the matter—but the transaction itself was established by the fact that it was witnessed by men of standing and trustworthy character in the community.

So that is the cultural context of this story. But even more important and relevant to the story is the character context of the story. In Ruth and Boaz, we have two people of sterling, godly character, and it is the beautiful, faithful character of these two lives that will awaken and energize the faith of the people around them. We see this principle first in the story of Boaz at the gate. The elders and men of the town see that Boaz has done a noble act in obedience to God: he has risked his love-relationship with Ruth in order to call the other kinsman to his responsibility—and then, when the other kinsman declined, Boaz took responsibility for both Ruth and Naomi, so that the line of Elimelech would continue. Seeing the faithfulness of Boaz, the men of the town affirmed Boaz and gave praise to God, saying:

> "We are witnesses. May the LORD make the woman who is coming into your home like Rachel and Leah, who together built up the house of Israel. May you have standing in Ephrathah and be famous in Bethlehem. Through the offspring the LORD gives you by this young woman, may your family be like that of Perez, whom Tamar bore to Judah."

Later, we will see a similar response by the women of the town to the faithful, godly character of Ruth. When God's people demonstrate honorable, righteous, unhypocritical character, the people around them are inspired and encouraged in their own faith, and give praise to God.

Redemption points to God

The story of Ruth is a story of redemption. God is in the redemption business. His priorities are completely unlike ours. While we praise and admire the successful, the winners, and the beautiful people, God reserves a special place in His vast heart for people who are needy, bruised, broken, forgotten, or failed. God receives glory when the lowly are lifted up, when the marginalized and forgotten are brought to the forefront and honored, when lives that are broken and destroyed are miraculously restored and created new. That is the heart of the gospel.

There's a telling implication in this story in Ruth chapter 4. The way the writer of the book treats the "close relative" is interesting and significant. The writer deliberately omits the name of the other kinsman. There is an odd word used in Ruth 4:1, where Boaz says, "Come over here, my friend, and sit down." The words "my friend" in the original Hebrew are a kind of fill-in-the-blank noun that suggests that Boaz actually said the man's name, but the writer does not quote the name in the text. So a better translation of the original Hebrew in this verse might be, "Come over here, so-and-so, and sit down."

The implication is that the writer of the book knew the man's name (certainly Boaz knew it), but the writer does not want the man's name to be recorded in history. It is as if the writer is saying, "Because of his irresponsibility in this situation, this man is not even worthy of being identified and remembered." Understand, the man's decision not to accept responsibility for widows and property was not especially wrong. He knew Boaz would act if he did not. The women would not be left uncared for.

But there is something a little disreputable about this man—some reason that the writer of Ruth has chosen to blot his name out of the story. I think it is reasonable to infer from the dialogue between Boaz and this man that the other kinsman was a man of rather questionable character and motives. It appears that this man does not think of his duty under the Law, nor of the family line and memory of Elimelech, or of the welfare of these two widows. His first thought seems to be for himself, and how he might use this situation to his advantage and personal enrichment. We can imagine a twinkle in his eye and a smile on his face as he initially embraces the idea.

But then Boaz tells him, "That's not all there is to this situation—you have a duty to marry the young widow and father a child by her, and you have a duty to raise that child under the family name of Mahlon and Elimelech. No property will be added to your family. You'll have all the responsibility and none of the advantages." At that moment, the twinkle in the man's eye fades and the smile on his face disappears. What seemed at first to be an opportunity is now only a burden to him—so he declines. Perhaps there was even an element of racism in the man's final decision. It is only after Boaz mentions "Ruth the Moabitess" that the man changes his mind.

This other kinsman declined to accept his lawful responsibilities because he did not look at life in a redemptive way. Unlike Boaz, he did not live his live in such a way as to be a channel of God's blessing to the lives of others. He saw only advantages and duties and deals and land and property, all the things that were part of the ordinary course of affairs. He could think only in those terms. It didn't occur to him that a Moabite widow might be someone God loves and cares about—nor did it occur to him that this woman from a foreign land might be a key element in God's plan for Israel and for the entire human race.

At the beginning of the book of Ruth, we are told the name of a minor character, a Moabitess named Orpah, who appears briefly, then returns to her land and her gods, and is never heard from again. Amazingly, though a minor character such as Orpah is identified by name, this kinsman—whose role in the story is pivotal—remains anonymous to this day. His name is blotted out of the story of Ruth because he didn't have the insight to see that God was working as a redeemer in the lives of His people.

So Boaz steps in and takes on the responsibility the other man has declined. He will make Ruth his wife, he will raise up and honor the name of Elimelech and Mahlon, he will take Mahlon's widow into his home and father the child to carry on Mahlon's name. In so doing, Boaz not only redeems the property of Elimelech and Naomi, he redeems the life of Ruth. This woman, who might have otherwise spent the rest of her life ignored and downtrodden, a poverty-stricken widow from a foreign land, has been given a new start in life by this Christlike man, Boaz. He lifts Ruth up and elevates her in the community. He confers a beautiful covering of honor and nobility upon her.

It is important to notice exactly what the men of the town are saying when they give praise to God and tell Boaz, "May God make Ruth to be like Rachel and Leah, and may He give you a son like Perez, whom Tamar bore to Judah." Who were Rachel, Leah, and Tamar? They were women with blemished, imperfect lives. In that ancient culture, it was a mark of shame for a married woman to be childless—and Rachel was a woman who went childless, decade after decade. Leah was the unattractive daughter, the unloved wife. Tamar was an outsider who had been treated terribly by Judah, her father-in-law, and was impregnated under false circumstances.

The stories of Rachel, Leah, and Tamar are stories of grief and tragedy—but they are ultimately stories of God's redemption. In each of these cases, God redeemed their lives and made these women objects of blessing and grace. So the men of the town gave credit to God for the fact that Ruth—a poor and rejected woman of Moab—had been lifted up and honored, just as these other women had been in times past.

The marriage of Ruth and Boaz

When Boaz declares that he will take Ruth as his wife, there is a universal acclaim, respect, and honor paid this couple by the elders and people of the city. Why did this honor come to Boaz and Ruth? Because they made a godly decision not to sell out or short-circuit God's plan. Ruth chose not to use a late-night seduction to accomplish God's goals, and Boaz did not press his advantage that night on the threshing floor. Instead, both Ruth and Boaz were willing to bet their future on the faithfulness of God. They chose to follow God's law and allow God to solve their problem for them.

A public marriage is an honorable and beautiful thing, an opportunity for the entire community to rejoice and thank God for what He intends to do in these two lives. Whenever I perform a wedding, I can't help but think of the adventure that these two people are embarking on—an adventure of trusting God and discovering what surprises He has for them around each bend in the road of life. At almost every wedding I perform, there are usually several people who are openly in tears. These are tears of rejoicing, as these witnesses think about the profound thing God is doing in joining this man and this woman together for life.

God never intended that marriages should take place furtively, quickly, or secretly. He created marriage as an event which should involve the entire community. Ruth and Boaz chose not to take the easy way; they chose not to spend a night of stolen lovemaking and secret bonding on the threshing floor; they chose not to ease the other kinsman out of the way. In the process of making that godly choice, they blessed the entire community, and brought rejoicing to the town. They demonstrated the goodness of God, and the whole town rejoiced over what God had done in bringing these two people together.

Ruth and Boaz demonstrated godly restraint and self-control. They refused to take advantage of the darkness, the secrecy, and the lowered barriers of the night-time party to become physically intimate. They didn't make promises with their bodies that they weren't free to keep for the rest of their lives. They realized that in order to be honorable, they had to obey God's law and approach the man who had first responsibility to do the right thing.

The relationship of Ruth and Boaz is instructive to us today. There are so many temptations in our time to cut corners, to hedge our bets, to sell out, to serve our own interests and forget God's will and the larger good. If Ruth and Boaz had chosen to do so, they could have cut corners and succeeded in getting married—but they wouldn't have demonstrated God's goodness and they wouldn't have been operating within God's will. Though they would have accomplished the same goal and gotten married either way, one choice would keep them within God's will while the other would take them outside of God's will. One way leads to greater character growth while the other is a retreat from character and obedience.

Even if the result of obedience does not bring us what we want, even if the risk that Boaz and Ruth took resulted in a loss of the relationship they wanted, obedience to God is still the better path. Following the instincts of the flesh may make you rich, or give you short-term success in relationships, or help you to achieve some other goal in life—but only following the will of God brings you character, honor, and the approval of God.

So the wedding that Boaz and Ruth had hoped for, and trusted God for, finally takes place. Ruth 4:13a tells us, "So Boaz took Ruth and she became his wife." There is no further description of their wedding. In fact, it may well be that when Boaz received the blessing of the elders of his town, the marriage was a done deal. But whether their marriage was simply recognized by the elders at the city gate, or whether there was a lavish celebration with food, wine, and dancing, it was a beautiful event. What made it beautiful was the fact that this was a union that was completely sanctioned and sanctified by God—and it was a celebration of the godly character of Boaz and Ruth.

Many of us can seem godly and pious on the outside. We can go to church and do our religious service and perform

157 The Infinite/Intimate God

our Christian acts—and still be completely phony on the inside. We can go to Bible studies and Christian retreats, we can sing the Christian songs with gusto and pray with eloquence—and it could all be a false front, like a façade on a Hollywood movie set. Other Christians will never know the difference. Only God would really know.

Ruth and Boaz could have made that kind of choice. They could have engaged in shortcuts and served their own interests in the dark of night, when no one was looking. But they chose instead to be faithful and obedient, even in private, when no one else could see. In the book of Ruth, we are given an opportunity to eavesdrop on this couple when no one else can see except God—and what is revealed to us is a godly couple, a righteous man and a righteous woman choosing to do the difficult thing, the obedient thing, in order to remain true to God.

Lord of the universe—and of the human heart

Every day, we see people around us who are completely unaware of God and His love for individual human beings. Some are successful, seemingly self-sufficient men and women who believe that they have achieved everything they have by their own strength. They do not recognize God's involvement in their lives, nor do they want anything to do with His love and His will. Others are the broken people of the world, sleeping in doorways or on sewer grates, surviving by panhandling or rummaging in trash cans, just marking time until they die. They don't believe God cares about them, and they don't care about God. Both the up-and-outers and the down-and-outers need to hear that the God of the universe is involved in individual human lives. They need to know that there is Love at the heart of the universe, and that this Love has come to earth in human form, and that this Love died on a cross for their sakes.

The story of Ruth and Boaz is the story of the Creator-God of the universe, reaching down to earth, responding to the obedience of two human beings, caring enough to be involved in directing the circumstances of their lives. When we think of what this really means—that there is a God who is both infinite and intimate, who directs the course of both a swirling galaxy and an individual human life—we are reminded of the words of David in Psalm 8:3–4:

> When I consider your heavens,
>   the work of your fingers,
> the moon and the stars,
>   which you have set in place,
> what is man that you are mindful of him,
>   the son of man that you care for him?

David reflected on the heavens and wondered, "Why would God pay attention to mere human beings? In the vast scheme of things, why would a tiny individual like me expect to gain God's attention or favor? What right have I to expect God to invest my life with significance and meaning?" But David doesn't stop there. He goes on to say,

> You made him a little lower than the
>   heavenly beings
>   and crowned him with glory and honor.
> You made him ruler over the works
>   of your hands;
>   you put everything under his feet . . . .

In other words, David is saying, "Even though a human being is lower in power and stature than the heavenly beings, God has exalted and honored human beings. For reasons known only to God, He has chosen to be involved in the lives of human beings."

God is Lord of the universe—and Lord of the human heart. He cares about cosmic events that span millions of light-years—and He cares about the feelings of two people in love.

The final verses of Ruth chapter 4 remind us that He was performing a powerful work through Boaz and Ruth, and that He chose to use their obedience to accomplish His eternal purpose. For those closing verses tell us that a child was born to Ruth and Boaz, and that child was in the line of the ancestry of King David. And Matthew chapter 1 tells us that Ruth, Boaz, and their child Obed were also in the line of the ancestry of King Jesus, the Messiah.

Ruth and Boaz could have served themselves, but instead they trusted and served God, and their choice of obedience became a fulcrum upon which all of human history turned. Out of their choice of obedience, God brought about the most important event in the history of the universe—the birth of the Savior, and through Him, the salvation of the world.

You and I never know just how important this or that moral choice may be. We never know how some small act of obedience on our part might reverberate and resonate, affecting others' lives for God's good. God always knows what He is doing, even though we do not always know. Our job is not to short-cut God's plans or help His plans along, as Naomi supposed, but to submit to His will and live in obedience to His Word. We cannot trust God and hedge our bets. We cannot trust God and the flesh at the same time. We must trust God, period!

From one point of view, the book of Ruth is a story about some small-town farm folk who fall in love. But from another point of view, it's the story about how two people's godliness and obedience affect the course of human history—and even the course of eternity. It's the story about how God can take the seemingly small acts and choices in our lives and magnify their effect millions of times over.

Because Ruth and Boaz trusted God, the Word became flesh and dwelt among us. The Lord of the cosmos came among us. He truly cares about us, whether we see ourselves as "heroes" or "zeros." He created time and He created space, and everything—the entire universe, the past, present, and future—belong to Him. We don't know what tomorrow may bring, but He knows what is to come in future millennia. Like Ruth and Boaz, we can trust Him—

And He will not disappoint us.

CHAPTER 10

A CHILD IS BORN

Ruth 4

There is probably no news more happily received than a birth announcement. Those little cherub-adorned greeting cards, trimmed either in blue or pink, spread excitement and joy that is completely disproportionate to the routine facts they relate—"It's a Boy (or Girl)! Baby so-and-so was born at a certain time on such-and-such date, weighing so-many pounds and ounces, measuring X number of inches in length." No big surprises there—but the news is thrilling nonetheless. A new life has entered the world. A new adventure has begun.

The last paragraph of the book of Ruth also contains a birth announcement. Upon this long-awaited child rests the hopes of an entire family:

> So Boaz took Ruth and she became his wife. Then he went to her, and the LORD enabled her to conceive, and she gave birth to a son. The women said to Naomi: "Praise be to the LORD, who this day has not left you without a kinsman-redeemer. May he become famous throughout Israel! He will renew your life and sustain you in your old age. For your daughter-in-law, who loves you and who is better to you than seven sons, has given him birth."

Then Naomi took the child, laid him in her lap and cared for him. The women living there said, "Naomi has a son." And they named him Obed. He was the father of Jesse, the father of David.

This, then, is the family line of Perez:

Perez was the father of Hezron,
Hezron the father of Ram,
Ram the father of Amminadab,
Amminadab the father of Nahshon,
Nahshon the father of Salmon,
Salmon the father of Boaz,
Boaz the father of Obed,
Obed the father of Jesse,
and Jesse the father of David.

Once again, as throughout the book of Ruth, we are confronted by a contrast between Ruth and Naomi. Though it was Ruth who gave birth to the boy Obed, both Ruth and Naomi were dramatically affected by the birth of this child. In fact, Naomi's life was so transformed that the women of the town proclaimed that a son had been born to Naomi! "Then Naomi took the child, laid him in her lap and cared for him," it says in verses 16 and 17. "The women living there said, 'Naomi has a son.' "

Growing in grace

A lesson can be drawn from the differences between the younger woman (a woman of simple trusting faith) and the older woman (who struggled and wrestled with God). These two women, Ruth and Naomi, were bound together by love, yet they experienced life differently. In the contrast between Ruth and Naomi, we as Christians learn a great deal about the choices we make every day that move us either closer to Christlike character or away from it.

In 2 Peter 3:18, the apostle tells us, "But grow in the grace and knowledge of our Lord and Savior Jesus Christ." This benediction, given to believers, encourages us with the knowledge that God desires our growth. He has made it possible for us to take the steps that lead to maturity. We can make decisions that move us toward Christlike character. Grace offers us an environment for growth. God honors the choices we make, and He enables us to become the people He created us to be.

That is the story of Ruth and Boaz. Each of them were apprehended by the grace of God early on, and day by day they grew in grace. On a regular, continual basis, they made the choices that produced godly character in their lives. And as a result of the lifelong preparation they have made, God brought them together as man and wife. The marriage took place, and they became parents—and these events were a direct outgrowth of their growth in grace. Maturity is not an arbitrary stroke of luck that happens to some people and not to others. Maturity is the logical, predictable consequence of our willingness to trust, follow, and obey the Lord. Our choices move us toward or away from maturity.

Boaz and Ruth chose the best way to experience God's grace: they willingly entrusted their lives to Him. But that is not the only way God dispenses His grace in our lives. Sometimes, His grace *captures* us against our will. Sometimes, we run from His grace, and He hounds us and tackles us with His grace despite our best efforts to elude Him and shake Him off. The apostle Paul was like that. He fought God and persecuted Christians until Jesus stopped him dead in his tracks on the road to Damascus. There, Paul was struck blind, knocked to his knees, and captured by God's grace.

That, in many ways, is the story of Naomi. This woman had suffered greatly and had become embittered against God. She resisted God's plan and distrusted His love and goodness in her life. She tried to circumvent His plan for her life. While

He tried to help her and meet her needs, she fought Him and wrestled with Him and blamed Him for all her suffering. But in the end, she was captured by God's grace.

A child is born

It is interesting to note that there is only one verse in Ruth 4 in which the narrative refers to Ruth herself, and that is verse 13 (she is also referred to in dialogue by Boaz in verses 5 and 10):

> So Boaz took Ruth and she became his wife. Then he went to her, and the LORD enabled her to conceive, and she gave birth to a son.

This verse doesn't give us much detail, but we don't need much. Here we find five short statements, one right after the other, which speak volumes: (1) Boaz took Ruth, (2) she became his wife, (3) he went to her, (4) the Lord enabled her to conceive, and (5) she gave birth to a son.

The first announcement is that Boaz took Ruth. Why does this statement need to be made? Because it makes clear that Ruth was able to leave her past behind. Ruth began this story as a former idolater, a daughter of Moab. She proceeded into childless widowhood—an extremely difficult circumstance, resulting in her extreme poverty. She was a foreigner. Her past was filled with personal struggle, but Boaz lifted her out of it. The past didn't dominate her future. She became the honored wife of an honorable man, a daughter of Israel, and a progenitor of Messiah.

Second, we are told that Ruth and Boaz were married. Now, under the law of the *levir*, Ruth and Boaz did not have to be in love in order to marry. A purely external, legal, loveless marriage would fulfill the requirements of the law. Boaz need do nothing more than acquire the widow, bring her into his home, and have a child by her. But the beautiful thing about this marriage was that Boaz truly loved Ruth, and she truly loved him. She was given the highest possible status in his world. He didn't just do the minimum of fulfilling the law—he did the maximum of embracing and loving this woman.

Third, this verse tells us that Boaz "went to her," meaning that they were lovers. They had a sexual relationship, a natural and beautiful physical expression of their love and emotional intimacy.

Fourth, the Lord enabled Ruth to conceive (I want to come back to this fact and explore it in greater detail in a moment).

Fifth, Ruth gave birth to a son. And, as we shall soon see, Ruth's son was, in a very real sense, Naomi's son as well. In verses 14–15, the women of the town of Bethlehem give praise to God:

> The women said to Naomi: "Praise be to the LORD, who this day has not left you without a kinsman–redeemer. May he become famous throughout Israel! He will renew your life and sustain you in your old age. For your daughter-in-law, who loves you and who is better to you than seven sons, has given him birth."

This is the second time in chapter 4 that we hear a chorus of praise from the townspeople of Bethlehem. The first time was the praise that the men at the gate voiced when Boaz announced that he would marry Ruth. This second expression of praise to God comes from the women of the town, because of the child who has been born to Ruth—and to Ruth's mother-in-law, Naomi. Both groups speak aloud in thanksgiving and recognition that God has been at work in an amazing way in the lives of Ruth and Boaz.

The praise and thanksgiving that the women voice in Ruth 4:14–15 is in vivid contrast to the scene in Ruth chapter

1, where Naomi insists to these same women, "Don't call me Naomi. Call me Mara, call me Bitterness, because I am a bitter woman living a bitter existence. God has turned against me." The bitterness of Naomi is drowned out at the end of the book by choruses of praise. All the women around Naomi remind her that God has not abandoned her.

In effect, these women seem to be saying to Naomi, "You were angry because you had no husband and no son, but you totally undervalued this young Moabite woman. She has been better to you than seven sons would have been. God has not left you alone. Do you realize how valuable Ruth is? Do you realize how thoroughly she contradicts your bitter, manipulative, and faithless spirit?"

And Naomi could not argue with these women. In fact, I suspect she no longer had any need of arguing. Instead of complaining, giving advice, and manipulating, I believe she sat down and bounced that beautiful baby on her knee while wearing the biggest, broadest smile anyone had ever seen!

There are few things that are more healing and refreshing to an aging heart than a grandchild. It is hard to be depressed when that little one places his hand in yours, when you hear his laughter, when you sense his joy as he discovers colors and shapes and music for the very first time. There's absolutely nothing like it. That is what Naomi got to experience when Ruth gave birth to Obed. Through this grandchild, the rays of God's light broke through the shroud of darkness Naomi had wrapped around herself.

Throughout this book, Naomi has served as a counterpoint and has stood in contrast to Ruth. Naomi has been hurt by her losses, her poverty, and her widowhood—and the pain of her existence has sunk deep into her heart. When life grows hard, Naomi grows hard in response. Ruth, on the other hand, seems to transcend it all. She is both outwardly and inwardly beautiful. You can almost hear the violins playing as she and the saintly Boaz are wed.

With Ruth, everything that ever happened in her life was completely in line with the kind of character and obedience she demonstrated. But Naomi struggled all the way through this story. She wrestled with God, railed at God, managed God, measured God, and trusted her own schemes rather than God's love and God's law—yet a son was born to her as well! And that is great news.

In the end, the focus of the story is not Boaz, not even Ruth. It is Naomi. The women of the village remind Naomi that this baby is going to become another *go'el* in her life. Eventually he will grow up, and Naomi will still live on the property that the family inherited, thanks to Boaz. Ultimately, when the baby Obed has grown to manhood, he will be the one to provide for Naomi.

Notice especially this line in verse 15: "For your daughter-in-law, who loves you and who is better to you than seven sons, has given him birth." The whole time Naomi has been frustrated and angry with God, feeling neglected and forgotten, crying out in her loneliness—she has not been alone at all! While Naomi lamented the fact that her husband and sons were dead, that there was no man in her life, she was never alone. There was a woman standing beside her who loved her.

Ruth has been better to Naomi than seven sons would have been. Ruth never abandoned her, and never stopped loving and supporting her. This embittered woman believed God's hand was against her, but she was never truly neglected. God's supply for her needs was there all along—but Naomi didn't see it.

Naomi gets to care for the baby at the end, and we see that her heart is changed in the process. Ultimately, nobody is left out, least of all Naomi. It isn't just heroic Ruth and noble Boaz who get drawn into the grace of God. Bitter, crabby old Naomi receives the full measure of God's grace as well. Ruth and Boaz never stub their toes in the whole story; Naomi stumbles through every scene! But that just goes to show that God's grace is for everyone—the faithful and the failing, the beautiful and the bitter, the godly and the gloomy. The Lord doesn't abandon anyone in the story. He brings blessing to Ruth, to Boaz, to Naomi—and through them, He blesses the entire town of Bethlehem.

Yahweh, the author of life and redemption

Let's return now to Ruth 4:13: "So Boaz took Ruth and she became his wife. Then he went to her, and the LORD enabled her to conceive, and she gave birth to a son." That is a significant statement.

Ruth and Boaz made choices and took obedient action—but it was the Lord who enabled Ruth to conceive and have a child. The word translated "LORD" in this passage is YHWH or Yahweh—God's personal name. The use of this name tells us that God was personally and actively taking a hand in helping Ruth and Boaz. This was not merely the laws of biology in action, but a deliberate act of God, enabling Ruth to conceive. This was not a routine conception.

It is important to remember that Ruth had been married once and hadn't given birth to a child. Now, since Boaz was an older man, it might even be less likely that she would be able to conceive. So it may be that the fact that this conception took place at all was a miracle of God.

But I would go a step further: I would suggest that there is no such thing as "routine" conception. God calls into being everyone who ever lives. These days, with all the procedures we have for treating infertility, including *in vitro* fertilization (bringing the egg and sperm together in a glass dish outside of the mother's body), it is often assumed that we're in complete control of the process of conception. If Ruth could have availed herself of the *in vitro* process, it might be said that the doctors enabled her to conceive, rather than the Lord.

But no matter how well we understand the science of conception, the Scriptures say that life comes from the Lord. He is the one who stamps His image onto human spirits that can respond to His Spirit. He is the one before whom we must make decisions about whether children will come into the world.

Our culture's confidence in medical technology has led to widespread acceptance of abortion on demand—even the gruesome practice of "partial birth abortion" during the latter stages of a pregnancy.

Yahweh is the Creator of life, and His heart is broken over the sin of abortion. He is the Eternal Judge, and I do not believe a nation which allows the slaughter of a million innocent lives year after year can escape His judgment. But He is also the Redeemer. His Son, Jesus, is the one who was nailed to a cross and prayed aloud, "Father, forgive them, for they do not know what they are doing."

I know that there will be some who read this book who have made the choice to end the life of a child by abortion. The same Yahweh who gives life also freely offers forgiveness and redemption. The same Yahweh who loves unborn children so much also loves His erring children, and He wants to take them off the path of death and set them on the path of life and righteousness. If we believe that God is at the heart of giving life, we must believe that he is at the heart of redeeming life. He calls each of us "Beloved." The taking of an innocent life is a terrible sin, but the love of Yahweh is deeper than our deepest sins.

Becky Pippert of InterVarsity Christian Fellowship tells the story of a friend, Sally, whom she led to Christ. After Sally's conversion, she began to experience horrible, all-consuming guilt over an abortion she had years earlier. In tears, Sally went to Becky and said, "A few years ago, I had an abortion and killed my baby. I don't see how God can ever forgive me!"

"Didn't you ask His forgiveness?" said Becky. "Didn't you ask Jesus to be your Lord and Savior? Well, He has done that. You are forgiven."

"I can't believe that—not after what I've done."

"Sally," she said, "you think of yourself as a murderer—and you're right. But that's not news. You were a murderer even *before* you had the abortion. And you know what? I'm a murderer, too! Every human being on the planet is a murderer. We all have innocent blood on our hands."

"Whose innocent blood?"

"The blood of Jesus," Becky answered. "Sally, we nailed Jesus Christ to the cross with our sins."

"I— I never looked at it that way."

"Sally," Becky continued, "God forgave us for killing His Son, Jesus. If He can forgive that, He can forgive you for having an abortion." When Sally realized the truth of that statement, she finally felt forgiven and at peace.

The greatest birth announcement of all

The final verses of Ruth 4 remind us that Boaz and Ruth had a powerful influence not only on their own time, but on ages to come. It was God's plan to use them as links in a chain that would fulfill His eternal purpose of redemption. In verses 18 to 22 we read:

> This, then, is the family line of Perez:
>
> Perez was the father of Hezron,
> Hezron the father of Ram,
> Ram the father of Amminadab,
> Amminadab the father of Nahshon,
> Nahshon the father of Salmon,
> Salmon the father of Boaz,
> Boaz the father of Obed,
> Obed the father of Jesse,
> and Jesse the father of David.

In the New Testament, Jesus the Messiah is often called "Son of David." Ruth and Boaz had no idea at the time that God was using them in such a mighty way, and that among their descendants would be King David of Israel as well as the Messiah, the King of Kings. They simply made the choice to trust and serve God, and they believed God would meet their needs. As a result, the most important event in the history of the universe—salvation—came about with their direct participation.

Remember the praise and rejoicing that is twice voiced by the community in Ruth chapter 4: First the men of Bethlehem say to Boaz, "May your house expand in Israel's history." Then the women of Bethlehem say to Ruth, "May this boy's name become famous in Israel." And those prayers are answered beyond anyone's ability to imagine!

The book of Ruth concludes with a genealogy, and you can almost hear a drumroll crescendo as each name is read: Perez, Hezron, Ram, Amminadab, Nahshon, Salmon, Boaz, Obed, Jesse, and—David! And it doesn't end with him, as great a king as he was. Biblical history tells us that this line continued all the way to the greatest King of all, the Messiah—

And, amazingly, the Messiah would be born right there in that same little town, the village of Bethlehem. The birth announcement of the Messiah would not come as a fancy greeting card with chubby little cherubs and a blue border. It would come from the mouths of angels. They would announce the birth of a great King—but His birth would take place in a stable. The child would be unknown and later rejected.

On that first Christmas, the world took no notice of the humble birth of Mary's little child. But that child was destined to become the Savior of the world.

You never know

No one really knows at the time what will one day prove to be important. Things that seem vitally important to us now will someday vanish into insignificance. Other things we scarcely notice today will one day be magnified beyond our ability to imagine.

A small act of kindness, a single prayer, a word of Christian testimony spoken at the right moment could be used by God to draw a person into God's kingdom—and that person may lead an entire family or hundreds of friends to Christ. An entire world could be transformed as a single act of kindness echoes and is magnified through the years and generations. During this very week as you are reading this book, people are ministering to children in Bible clubs and Sunday schools, never knowing whether or not one of those children might grow up to become the next Billy Graham or Joni Eareckson Tada, the next C. S. Lewis or Charles Swindoll, the next Amy Grant or Johann Sebastian Bach.

The same is true of those who offer a cup of cold water in Jesus' name, who visit prisoners, or who care for the poor. You never know what a single godly act today might produce in the future—or in eternity. None of us knows what the future holds—but we know who holds the future. God delights in using ordinary people who are yielded and obedient, and who trust His purposes and plan for their lives.

The two most wonderful and practical lessons that flow from this final paragraph of Ruth are these:

(1) You can either grow in grace—or you can be captured by grace. The choice is yours—but whichever you choose, God's grace is bigger than all of us. We can choose to live productive, godly, obedient lives like Ruth, or like Naomi we can gripe and complain as we are dragged, kicking and screaming, into the light of God's love.

(2) God chooses simple, ordinary, yielded, obedient people who don't see themselves as particularly significant or special in order to create the future and change the world.

Clearly, there is nothing out of the ordinary about you and me. We're just plain and simple folk, just like Ruth and

Boaz. So what are we waiting for? Let's trust God! Let's obey Him and keep ourselves in the very center of His eternal plan. You never know, He just might have a job for us to do—

And a world for us to change.

NOTES

Chapter 1:

1. John Leo, "A No-Fault Holocaust," *U.S. News & World Report*, July 21, 1997, p. 14, electronically retrieved at http://www.elibrary.com.

Chapter 8:

1. Barbara Reynolds, "90's Women More Than Sex Machines," *USA Today*, March 8, 1996, p. 12A.

Chapter 9:

1. Quoted by John Boslough in *Stephen Hawking's Universe* (New York: William Morrow & Co., 1985), p. 121.
2. Leonard Shlain, *Art and Physics* (New York: William Morrow & Co., 1991), p. 252.
3. (New York: Simon & Schuster, 1983), pp. 167–168.

Note to the Reader

The publisher invites you to share your response to the message of this book by writing Discovery House Publishers, Box 3566, Grand Rapids, MI 49501, USA. For information about other Discovery House books, music, or videos, contact us at the same address or call 1-800-653-8333. Find us on the Internet at http://www.dhp.org/ or send e-mail to books@dhp.org.